VIETNAM

2025

Vietnam Explorer 2025: Adventure, Nature, and Culture

Rocky C. Primo

Copyright © 2024 by Rocky C. Primo
All rights reserved. No part of this publication may be reproduced, stored or
transmitted in any form or by any means, electronic, mechanical,
photocopying, recording, scanning, or otherwise without written permission
from the publisher. It is illegal to copy this book, post it to a website, or
distribute it by any other means without permission.
Rocky C. Primo asserts the moral right to be identified as the author of this work.

Table of Contents

Chapter 1: Introduction to Vietnam
    Synopsis of History and Society
    The Climate and Geography
    Reasons to Go to Vietnam in 2025?
    Important Travel Advice and Information

Chapter 2: Planning Your Trip
    The Best Times to Go
    Visas and Requirements for Entry
    Concerns for Health and Safety
    Planning Your Travel Budget

Chapter 3: Hanoi – The Capital City
    The Best Things to Do in Hanoi
    Monuments and History Centres
    Dietary and Nutrition Guide
    Shopping and After Dark

Chapter 4: The Northern Highlands
    Sapa and its Adjacent Area
    Adventure and Trekking Pursuits
    Perspectives on Culture: Ethnic Minorities
    Places to Stay and Eat
    Tips for Highland Travel

Chapter 5: Ha Long Bay and Cat Ba Island
    A Visit to HaLong Bay: Boats and Tours
    Things to Do on Cat Ba Island

Eco-Friendly Vacation Advice

Chapter 6: Central Vietnam
   Hue the Imperial City in the past
   Hoi An: A Charming Old Town
   Beaches and Contemporary Attractions in Da Nang
   Son of Mine: Historic Ruins
   Cultural Celebrations and Occasions

Chapter 7: Vietnam's Hidden Gems
   Off-the-Beaten-Path Destinations
   Lesser-Known Cultural Experiences
   Unique Activities and Adventures
   Local Insights and Tips

Frequently asked questions

Conclusion

Chapter 1: Introduction to Vietnam

Southeast Asian country Vietnam is well-known for its varied culture, long history, and breathtaking scenery. Vietnam presents a singular fusion of the ancient and the modern, from the peaceful countryside to the busy cities. After overcoming colonization and conflict to become a thriving and dynamic travel destination, the nation's history is characterized by tenacity and perseverance.

Vietnam's borders are the South China Sea, China, Laos, and Cambodia. It is situated geographically along the eastern edge of the Indochinese Peninsula. There are many different environments to explore due to the climate's variation from the temperate north to the tropical south.

Vietnam's stunning natural beauty, which includes the meditative beaches of Da Nang and Nha Trang, the mysterious limestone islands of Ha Long Bay, and the terraced rice fields of Sapa, is what draws tourists there. There are many cultural treasures to be found, such as the well-preserved architecture of the ancient town of Hoi An and the imperial citadels and royal tombs of the historical capital of Hue.

Vietnam travel is a sensory experience as well as an adventure. The cuisine is well-known, with meals like banh mi, pho, and fresh spring rolls providing a mouthwatering taste of regional flavors. Vietnam is a must-see destination in 2025 because of its welcoming people, lively markets, and colorful festivals, all of which enhance the travel experience.

Synopsis of History and Society

Vietnam has a remarkably resilient and rich cultural history spanning thousands of years. Early societies, such as the Dong Son culture, established the groundwork for a society that would withstand multiple periods of foreign rule. Vietnamese culture was greatly impacted by more than a millennium of Chinese rule, especially in terms of language, religion, and government.

With notable wins over the Chinese and Mongols, the Vietnamese successfully resisted numerous invasions. French colonization brought Western influences and ignited a powerful independence movement in the 19th century. This resulted in the Vietnam War and other wars that shaped modern Vietnam, culminating in Ho Chi Minh's declaration of independence in 1945.

Vietnamese culture today is a well-balanced fusion of native customs and outside influences. Deep respect for family and community is shared by Taoism, Buddhism, and

Confucianism. Vietnamese culture is deeply ingrained in festivals, traditional music, and dance, which all serve to highlight the country's resilient character and rich cultural legacy.

The Climate and Geography

Vietnam's terrain is varied, encompassing more than 1,000 miles from north to south along the Indochinese Peninsula's eastern border. The nation has a vast coastline that runs along the South China Sea, as well as a variety of mountain ranges and river deltas.

Vietnam's northern region is known for its untamed mountains and the lush Red River Delta, which is home to the country's capital, Hanoi. With four distinct seasons—cold winters and hot, muggy summers—this region has a subtropical climate.

The stunning coastal plains and the Annamite Range are located in central Vietnam. This area is well-known for its breathtaking beaches and important historical sites, such as Hue and Hoi An. This region has a tropical climate, with a distinct rainy season that runs from September to December and is frequently accompanied by typhoons.

The vast Mekong Delta and the energetic city of Ho Chi Minh City are located in southern Vietnam. The two main seasons in this region's tropical climate are the rainy season, which runs from May to October, and the dry season, which runs from November to April. All year long, the weather is pleasant, which makes it the perfect place to explore the lush delta and exciting city life.

Travelers can experience a wide range of activities in Vietnam due to its diverse geography and climate, from sunny beaches and bustling cities to trekking in the country's northern highlands.

Reasons to Go to Vietnam in 2025?

Vietnam in 2025 promises a travel experience like no other, combining vibrant culture, rich history, and breathtaking natural beauty. The nation's upgraded infrastructure, wide range of tourist attractions, and friendly people are making it a popular travel destination for visitors from around the world.

Vietnam's continuous modernisation and development make 2025 a great year to visit the country. New cultural venues, better public transport, and a developing culinary scene can be found in cities like Hanoi and Ho Chi Minh City. Furthermore, 2025 will commemorate the 50th anniversary of Vietnam's reunification, with a wide range of national events and celebrations scheduled to offer a distinctive window into Vietnamese culture.

The nation's natural areas are more approachable than before thanks to increased ecotourism programs that encourage environmentally friendly travel. Vietnam offers a remarkable variety of landscapes, ranging from the pristine beaches of Phu Quoc to the karst formations of Ha Long Bay and Sapa's terraced rice fields.

Vietnam's affordability is still a big lure, too. From opulent lodging to delectable street cuisine, travelers can have top-notch experiences without going over budget.

When you travel to Vietnam in 2025, you will experience a vibrant fusion of modernity and tradition, seeing a country that respects its history while looking to the future. It's a journey that will leave you with priceless memories and life-changing experiences.

Important Travel Advice and Information

Visas and Requirements for Entry
Visa Requirements: In order to enter Vietnam, most visitors need a visa. For a single 30-day entry, you can apply online for an e-visa.
Certain nationalities are exempt from requiring a visa for brief visits. Visit the Vietnamese consulates or embassies to view the most recent information.

Security and Health

Immunisations: Make sure your regular immunisations are current. Precautions for typhoid, malaria, and hepatitis A are advised.

Health Insurance: It's crucial to have travel insurance that includes health coverage. Make sure medical evacuations are covered by your policy.

Vietnam is generally safe, but keep an eye out for small-time theft, particularly in populated areas. Keep valuables in hotel safes.

Funds and Expenses

Currency: The local unit of currency is the Vietnamese Dong (VND). In cities, ATMs are commonly found.

Budgeting: Vietnam is reasonably priced. While local transport and street food can be reasonably priced, prices in tourist areas can differ greatly.

The official language of communication is Vietnamese. In tourist areas, English is widely spoken.

Connectivity: SIM cards with data are inexpensive and can be found in large cities and airports.

Transport

Domestic Travel: Vietnam's domestic bus, train, and airline networks are well-connected. Ride-sharing apps and motorbike taxis are popular for short trips.

Operating a motorbike: It's usual to rent one, but make sure you have the required licenses and drive carefully.

Customary Protocols

Honor customs When visiting places of worship, dress modestly. Shoes must be taken off when entering temples and homes.

Social Customs: Use both hands when giving and receiving objects, and refrain from touching people's heads.

Packing Suggestions

Clothing for the Climate: If you're traveling somewhere colder than the tropics, bring warmer layers; otherwise, pack light, breathable clothing.

Bring a reusable water bottle, sunscreen, and insect repellent as essentials.

You'll be ready for an unforgettable and trouble-free trip to Vietnam in 2025 with these pointers and crucial information.

Chapter 2: Planning Your Trip

Organizing Your Journey
Best Season to Travel: Spring (March to May): Known for its moderate temperatures nationwide, this season is excellent for traveling to both the north and south of the country.
Autumn (September to November): Perfect for visiting cities and natural settings, with pleasant temperatures and less rainfall.
Preparing for Typhoon Season: If you're traveling to Central Vietnam, make sure you have plans for typhoons, which typically occur from September to December.
Visas and Entry Requirements
E-Visa: Good for a single 30-day entry, available to nationals of many nations. Via the official government website, submit an online application.
At major airports, a pre-approval letter from a Vietnamese travel agency is required for obtaining a visa on arrival.
Exemptions from Visas: Certain nationalities are permitted entry without a visa for brief visits. The regulations are subject to change, so it is always advisable to double check.
Considerations for Health and Safety
Vaccinations: For some areas, the prophylactic administration of malaria, typhoid, and hepatitis A are advised. Everyday immunisations ought to be current.

Health Insurance: Having complete travel insurance is crucial, as it should cover medical evacuation.

Travelers should feel safe in Vietnam overall. Take the customary safeguards against small-time theft, especially in crowded areas. Don't show off your valuables and make use of reliable transit services.

Setting Up Your Travel Accommodation Budget: Vietnam offers a wide range of accommodations, from luxurious resorts to inexpensive hostels. The average daily cost can vary greatly, from $20 to more than $150, based on your preferences.

Food: You can get delicious and reasonably priced street food for as little as $1–$3. Mid-range eateries usually charge between $5 and $15 per meal.

Transportation: Cheap domestic flights, trains and buses are available. A cheap way to see the area is by renting a motorbike.

Suggested Routes of Travel

Typical Route: Hanoi – Ha Long Bay – Hue – Hoi An – Da Nang – Ho Chi Minh City – Mekong Delta (2 weeks).

Cultural Tour (10 Days): Sapa, Hanoi, Ninh Binh, Hoi An, Hue, and Ho Chi Minh City.

Two weeks of nature and adventure: Phong Nha-Ke Bang National Park, Ha Long Bay, Central Highlands, and Mekong Delta; Northern Highlands (Sapa).

Essentials of Packing

Clothes: Layers for colder climates in the north, light, breathable clothing for tropical climates. dress modestly in rural areas and at temples.

Sandals and cosy walking shoes are appropriate footwear.

Health items: A simple first aid kit, sunscreen, and insect repellent.
Documents: Copies of all relevant paperwork, such as flight schedules, passports, and visas.
Communication and Networking
SIM cards are reasonably priced and accessible at convenience stores and airports. Vinaphone, Mobifone, and Viettel are a few of the major suppliers.
Language: In tourist areas, most people speak and understand basic English. Acquiring a few Vietnamese phrases can be beneficial and valued.
Taking these things into account will make your trip planning easier and guarantee that your 2025 trip to Vietnam is enjoyable and unforgettable.

The Best Times to Go

The Best Times to Go
Vietnam's climate varies greatly from north to south, so it's crucial to organize your trip around the areas you want to see. Below is a summary of the ideal periods to travel to various regions of the nation:

Northern Vietnam: Sapa, Ha Long Bay, and Hanoi
Spring: from March to May Perfect for trekking in Sapa and touring the energetic city of Hanoi, this time of year offers pleasant temperatures and blooming flowers. Clear skies and

tranquil waters make Ha Long Bay an ideal destination for cruises.

Autumn: September through November is a great time to go because of the nice weather and lower humidity. The harvest season in the northern highlands provides breathtaking views, and the landscapes are lush following the summer rains.

Central Vietnam (Hue, Da Nang, Hoi An): February through May: Warm, dry weather makes these months ideal for hanging out on Da Nang's beaches, discovering Hoi An, an ancient town, and touring Hue's historical sites.

Stay away from September through December: During these months, this region is vulnerable to typhoons and heavy rains, which can cause travel plans to be disrupted and outdoor activities to be limited.

Dry season (November to April) in southern Vietnam (Ho Chi Minh City, Mekong Delta, Phu Quoc): ideal travel season due to mild temperatures and little rain. This time is ideal for taking leisurely strolls along the Phu Quoc beaches, exploring the busy streets of Ho Chi Minh City, and cruising the Mekong Delta.

Avoid the rainy season, which runs from May through October. It is marked by a lot of humidity and frequent showers. Though there may be fewer visitors and more verdant, lush scenery during this time of year, if you don't mind the rain.

Extra Attention to Detail

Tet Festival: Usually taking place in late January or early February, Tet is the Lunar New Year. This is a lively and culturally diverse time to visit, but be ready for peak travel times as locals travel far and wide on this holiday.

You can guarantee a more comfortable and pleasurable experience while taking in Vietnam's varied landscapes and attractions by scheduling your trip to coincide with the best weather windows for each area.

Visas and Requirements for Entry

Visa Qualifications
Citizens of more than 80 nations, including many European nations, the United States, Canada, the United Kingdom, and Australia, can apply for an e-visa. Applying online via the official Vietnamese government website, the e-visa is good for a single 30-day entry.

Tourists can obtain a visa upon arrival at major airports in Da Nang, Ho Chi Minh City, and Hanoi for travel by air. Prior to your arrival, a pre-approval letter from a Vietnamese travel agency is required. Normally, this kind of visa is only good for 30 days, but it can be extended.

Exemptions from Visas: Nationals of a few countries, including South Korea, Japan, and some ASEAN nations, are not required to obtain a visa for visits that last no more than 15 to 30 days. The exclusion list is subject to change, so make sure to check the most recent version.

Application Procedure
E-Visa: Go to the e-Visa portal maintained by the Vietnamese government.

Provide your travel itinerary, personal information, and a passport photo when completing the application form.

Online, pay the non-refundable fee (about $25 USD).

Await approval and the processing period, which typically takes three business days, before downloading your e-visa.

Visa on Arrival: Use a duly authorized Vietnamese travel agency or visa service to apply for a visa approval letter.

Get the approval letter through email (it takes two to three business days to process requests).

Provide your approval letter, passport photos, filled-out entry/exit form, and the stamping fee (between $25 and $50 USD) at the visa on arrival counter when you arrive in Vietnam.

The requirements for a passport

Validity: The minimum amount of time your passport is valid is six months after the date you intend to enter Vietnam.

Pages without text: Make sure you have two unfilled pages in your passport so that your visa can be stamped. Health and Travel Insurance

Health Insurance: Having travel insurance that pays for medical costs, including repatriation and evacuation, is advised.

Vaccinations: While not required, it is advisable to stay up to date on routine vaccines as well as those for typhoid and hepatitis A. Other vaccinations, such as Hepatitis B and malaria prophylaxis, may be advised based on the area and activities.

Regulations Regarding Customs

Prohibited Items: A few things are off limits completely, including weapons, drugs, and porn.

Allowances for Duty-Free Shopping: Guests are permitted to import 200 cigarettes, 1.5 litres of alcohol, and either 3 kg or 5 kg of tea or coffee duty-free. Duties may be applied to amounts over these caps.

Conditions for Departure

The cost of your airline ticket includes the departure tax, so you won't need to pay it separately at the airport.

Exit Visa: You have to apply for an exit visa at the immigration office before leaving Vietnam if you have overstayed your visa.

A hassle-free and easy trip can be facilitated by being aware of Vietnam's entry requirements and making sure all required documentation is in order.

Concerns for Health and Safety

Safety Measures for Health

Immunisations: Make sure your regular immunisations are current. Hepatitis A, typhoid, and, in certain situations, Japanese encephalitis are among the vaccinations advised for visitors visiting Vietnam. Think about getting malaria prophylaxis depending on your itinerary, especially if you're going to the Mekong Delta or rural areas.

Food Safety and Water Quality: Skip the tap water and instead sip boiling or bottled water. Recognise that ice cubes might contain tap water, so handle them with caution. Savour the food on the street, but pick busy, high-turnover stalls to guarantee freshness.

To protect yourself from mosquito-borne illnesses like dengue fever and malaria, wear long sleeves, sleep under a mosquito net if you're in a rural area, and use insect repellent that contains DEET.

Insurance and Medical Facilities

Medical Facilities: Reputable hospitals and clinics, many with staff fluent in English, can be found in major cities like Hanoi and Ho Chi Minh City. Medical facilities might be scarce in rural areas.

Travel Insurance: Having a thorough policy is crucial. Make sure it includes evacuation, medical care, and repatriation. Verify if your insurance covers everything you intend to do, including riding a motorbike or participating in adventure sports.

Tips for Safety

Petty Theft: Use caution in crowded places and popular tourist destinations. Store your valuables safely, and don't show off pricey things like jewelry and cameras. Keep passports and other important documents in hotel safes.

Scams: Be on the lookout for typical con games, like overcharging by cab drivers or vendors, and always settle on a price before taking services. For tours and transportation, go with reliable companies.

Safety in Traffic: Vietnamese traffic can be quite chaotic. Make sure you are familiar with riding in congested areas and possess an international driving permit before renting a motorbike. Don a helmet at all times. For a safer alternative to public transit, think about utilizing ride-sharing apps like Grab.

Emergency Numbers
Emergency Contact Numbers:
Officers: 113
Fire: 114
Ambulance: 115

Information from the Embassy: Remember the phone number of the embassy or consulate of your nation in Vietnam. If a passport is lost or there is an emergency, they can help.

Unnatural Catastrophes
Flooding and typhoons: From September to December, Central Vietnam is vulnerable to both flooding and strong storms. Pay attention to local advisories and stay up to date on weather conditions. If your travel schedule is disrupted, have a backup plan.

Earthquakes: Vietnam is susceptible to earthquakes, despite their rarity. Learn the proper protocols for handling earthquakes, particularly if you are going to a northern location.

Local Rules and Practices
Observe Local Laws: Become familiar with the laws and customs of the area. Drug offenses carry harsh penalties, and engaging in activities like gambling outside of casinos with licenses is prohibited.

Cultural Awareness: When visiting temples and rural areas, wear modest clothing. In general, it's not appropriate to show affection in public. Before taking pictures of people, always get their consent, especially from monks and members of ethnic minorities.

You can travel to Vietnam in 2025 in safety and comfort if you keep these health and safety factors in mind.

Planning Your Travel Budget

Options for Budget Accommodations: Hostels charge $5 to $15 per night for dorm beds. Most low-cost hotels and guesthouses have nightly rates between $15 and $30.

Mid-Range: A cozy hotel with good amenities can set you back between $30 and $70 a night. This range includes boutique hotels in popular locations.

Luxury: Nightly rates at upscale hotels and resorts start at $100 and go up to $300 or more. These provide first-rate amenities, prime locations, and superior services.

Eatery and Beverage

Street Food: Meals from this delicious and reasonably priced menu range from $1 to $3. Popular foods include bun cha, pho, and banh mi.

Local Restaurants: The price range for meals at local restaurants is $3 to $10. Try a variety of regional specialities; Vietnamese cuisine is diverse.

Mid-Range Restaurants: Mid-range restaurants serve a variety of regional and international dishes for $10 to $25 a meal.

High-End Dining: A great meal in a big city can set you back $25 to $50 or more per person. These eateries provide upscale fare in a refined setting.

Drinks: $1 to $2 local beer is a good deal. Vietnamese coffee is sold in coffee shops for $1 to $3, and fresh fruit juices can be purchased for about $1 everywhere. In bars and clubs, the cost of imported alcohol and cocktails can vary from $5 to $15.

Transport

Local Transportation: City bus fares usually start at less than $1, making buses the most economical choice. Motorbike and vehicle services are provided at affordable prices by ride-sharing apps such as Grab, ranging from $1 to $5 for brief journeys.

Traveling between major cities within the same country can cost anywhere from $30 to $100 based on the season and time of year you book. Depending on the class and distance, sleeper train tickets can cost anywhere from $20 to $70, making train travel a picturesque option.

Renting a motorbike is a common way for people to travel. $5 to $10 is the daily rental fee; however, make sure you have the required insurance and license.

Taxis: Metered taxis are accessible in urban areas, with starting prices of roughly $0.50 and $0.50 per kilometer.

Activities & Sightseeing Admission Fees: There are admission fees for popular tourist destinations that range from $1 to $15. A day cruise around HaLong Bay, for instance, can run you anywhere from $30 to $50, while the War Remnants Museum in Ho Chi Minh City costs about $2.

Excursions and Tours: Costs for scheduled tours differ. Day trips usually cost between $20 and $50, while multi-day tours can cost between $100 and $500, depending on the services and itinerary.

Recreational Activities: Adventure sports, boat tours, and cooking classes come in a wide range of prices. Spend between $10 and $50 on each activity.

Extraneous Charges

Shopping: Markets and shops offer apparel, handicrafts from the area, and souvenirs. Prices vary and bargaining is common.

Tipping is not required, but it is greatly appreciated. 10% is the typical tip for courteous service provided by drivers and tour guides, or in restaurants.

Internet and SIM cards: SIM cards that come with data plans are inexpensive, costing between $5 and $10 per month.

Daily Estimates of the Budget

Traveler on a tight budget: $30 to $50 per day (housing in dorms, dining on street food, utilizing public transportation).

Mid-Range Traveler: $50 to $100 per day (dining at neighborhood eateries, lodging in mid-range hotels, and occasionally taking tours).

Luxury Traveler: $150 to $300 or more per day (private tours and activities, fine dining at restaurants, and accommodations in upscale hotels).

You can have a pleasant and unforgettable trip to Vietnam in 2025 if you plan your budget appropriately.

Chapter 3: Hanoi – The Capital City

summary

Vietnam's capital city, Hanoi, is a city where modernity and tradition coexist harmoniously. Hanoi offers a distinctive fusion of old and new and is well-known for its colonial architecture, lively culture, and rich history. From the vibrant markets of the Old Quarter to the tranquil surroundings of Hoan Kiem Lake, the city's streets are a hive of activity.

Principal Attractions

Old Quarter: The bustling markets, winding streets, and traditional architecture of this historic district are well-known. The Dong Xuan Market and St. Joseph's Cathedral are important locations.

Hoan Kiem Lake is a major landmark encircled by lively streets and lovely parks. The lake provides a peaceful haven from the bustle of the city and is home to the Ngoc Son Temple.

Temple of Literature: Honoring Confucius, this country's first university offers insights into Vietnam's rich educational history through its exquisite gardens and historic architecture.

Vietnam's most revered leader, Ho Chi Minh, is remembered and honored at the Ho Chi Minh Mausoleum, a significant historical site. The Ho Chi Minh Museum and the Presidential Palace are also located within the complex.

Through exhibits and cultural artifacts, the Vietnam Museum of Ethnology offers a thorough look at the various ethnic groups that make up Vietnam.

Museums and Historical Sites

Vietnamese sculptures, paintings, and ceramics are on display at the Vietnam Fine Arts Museum, which also features modern and traditional Vietnamese artwork.

The "Hanoi Hilton," also known as the Hoa Lo Prison Museum, provides an insightful look at Vietnam's colonial past and the experiences of prisoners during the Vietnam War.

Impressive archaeological discoveries and insights into Hanoi's imperial past can be found at the Imperial Citadel of Thang Long, a UNESCO World Heritage site.

Cuisine and Eating

Hanoi is well-known for its street food culture. Vietnamese noodle soup (pho), grilled pork with noodles (bun cha), and Vietnamese baguettes (banh mi) are must-try foods.

Eat at local restaurants such as Quan An Ngon, which serves a variety of Vietnamese specialities, or Cha Ca La Vong, which serves traditional fish dishes.

Cafés: The café scene in Hanoi is very lively. Try the egg coffee at Cafe Giang, or sip on traditional iced Vietnamese coffee at neighborhood cafés near Hoan Kiem Lake.

Purchasing and Entertainment

Markets: You may buy local goods, apparel, and souvenirs at the Old Quarter's thriving markets, including Dong Xuan Market and Hanoi Weekend Night Market.

Boutiques and Art Galleries: See the Old Quarter's boutiques and art galleries to find one-of-a-kind textiles, artwork, and handicrafts.

Nightlife: There are many bars, clubs, and live music venues in Hanoi's bustling nightlife district. Ta Hien Beer Street and the Hanoi Opera House are well-liked locations for cultural events.

Day Trips Leaving From Hanoi
Famous for its breathtaking limestone karsts and emerald waters, Halong Bay is a UNESCO World Heritage site. Both overnight cruises and day trips are very popular.
Trekking and cultural experiences can be had in Sapa, which is well-known for its stunning scenery and villages home to ethnic minorities.
Ninh Binh: Often called "Halong Bay on land," Ninh Binh is home to striking karst scenery as well as ancient sites like Hoa Lu's capital.
Hanoi is a fascinating travel destination because of its unique blend of historical significance, cultural richness, and dynamic modern living.

The Best Things to Do in Hanoi

Top Hanoi Attractions
Old Quarter
The historic district of Hanoi is characterized by its traditional architecture and winding streets. There are artisanal shops, street food vendors, and busy markets all over the place.
Highlights include the street food vendors, Ma May Street, traditional craft stores, and Dong Xuan Market.

Hoan Kiem Lake
A picturesque lake nestled amidst parks and historical landmarks in the heart of the city. This location is well-liked for recreational and cultural pursuits.

Highlights include the island-based Ngoc Son Temple, the Turtle Tower, and the lovely walking trails around the lake.

Temple of Words
Confucius is the patron saint of Vietnam's first university. There are peaceful gardens and well-preserved architecture at the temple.
The Well of Heavenly Clarity, the Five Courtyards, and the stone stelae bearing the names of doctorate laureates are the highlights.

Mausoleum of Ho Chi Minh
This is a large mausoleum honoring the revolutionary leader of Vietnam, Ho Chi Minh. The Ho Chi Minh Museum and the Presidential Palace are located within the complex.
Highlights include the Ho Chi Minh Stilt House, the mausoleum itself, and the surrounding gardens.

Museum of Ethnology in Vietnam
This museum features artifacts and exhibits that highlight the cultures of the various ethnic groups that make up Vietnam.
Highlights include the ethnic artifacts, traditional clothing, and outdoor displays of traditional homes.

The Museum of Hoa Lo Prison

Known historically as the "Hanoi Hilton," this location saw use both during the Vietnam War and the French colonial era. It provides information about the stormy past of Vietnam.
Highlights: Historical exhibits, pictures of important occasions, and exhibits on prisoner conditions.

Thang Long's Imperial Citadel
Description: Remaining ruins of Hanoi's 11th-century old citadel can be found at this UNESCO World Heritage site.
The historical significance of the site, along with the ancient walls and archaeological artifacts, are the highlights.

Vietnam Museum of Fine Arts
A museum featuring both traditional and modern artwork from Vietnam's artistic past.
Highlights: Collections of ceramics, paintings, and sculptures that illustrate different eras and forms of Vietnamese art.

Cathedral of St. Joseph
French-built in the early 20th century, this neo-Gothic cathedral is evocative of Notre Dame in Paris.
Highlights: The elaborate interior details, the windows with stained glass, and the striking façade.

The Museum of Hoa Lo Prison
Often referred to as the "Hanoi Hilton," this historical prison provides visitors with an overview of Vietnam's colonial and military past through exhibits and parts of the facility that have been preserved.

Highlights include the historical background of the prison, the conditions of incarceration, and prominent figures from history.

Hanoi is a fascinating travel destination because of these attractions, which provide an in-depth look at the city's rich history, lively culture, and stunning architecture.

Monuments and History Centres

Museums and Historical Sites in Hanoi
Mausoleum of Ho Chi Minh
This imposing edifice honors Ho Chi Minh, the pioneer of Vietnam's independence movement. For paying respects and learning about Ho Chi Minh's legacy, the mausoleum is a significant location.

The mausoleum structure, Ho Chi Minh's stilt house, and the museum showcasing his life and contributions are the highlights.

The Museum of Hoa Lo Prison
During the Vietnam War, the French colonialists and the North Vietnamese both utilized this prison, which is also referred to as the "Hanoi Hilton." It provides insight into the challenging circumstances that prisoners endure.

Highlights: A section devoted to the experiences of American POWs, historical photographs, and exhibits on prisoner conditions.

Temple of Words
Founded in 1070, this university is the first in Vietnam. The Confucius-focused temple is a significant historical and cultural landmark.
Highlights include the Well of Heavenly Clarity, the Temple of Confucius, and the Five Courtyards. Additionally, the location has stelae bearing doctorate laureates' names.

Thang Long's Imperial Citadel
The political hub of Vietnam for more than a thousand years, this site is recognised as a UNESCO World Heritage site. The remains of the citadel provide a window into Hanoi's prehistoric past.
Highlights include the historic walls, the archaeological discoveries, and the Flag Tower, which provides sweeping views of Hanoi.

Museum of Ethnology in Vietnam
This museum features a vast array of exhibits and artefacts that offer a comprehensive look at the various ethnic groups that make up Vietnam.
Highlights: Ordinary objects, traditional ethnic house displays outdoors, and traditional costumes.

Vietnam Museum of Fine Arts
This museum showcases both traditional and contemporary art, honouring Vietnam's rich artistic legacy.
Highlights: A selection of traditional and well-known Vietnamese artists' creations, as well as sculptures, paintings, and ceramics.

Cathedral of St. Joseph
French-built in the early 20th century, this neo-Gothic cathedral is evocative of Notre Dame in Paris. It is a famous building in Hanoi's architecture.
Highlights: Stained glass windows, the elaborate interior design, and the façade of the cathedral.

Vietnamese National Museum of History
This museum provides a thorough overview of Vietnam's history from antiquity to the present and is housed in a building from the colonial era.
Points of interest include historical displays about the French colonial era, dynasty exhibits about Vietnam, and artifacts from ancient civilisations.

Temple Bach
One of the oldest temples in Hanoi, honoring the White Horse deity who, so myth tells us, aided in the founding of the city's first settlement.
Highlights: The temple's cultural significance, historical inscriptions, and traditional architecture.
10. Hoan Kiem Lake and the Temple of Ngoc Son
Hoan Kiem Lake is famous for its scenery, but it's also historically significant because it houses the Ngoc Son Temple, which is located on an island that can be reached by a charming red bridge.
Highlights: The scenic lake environment, the Turtle Tower, and the historical artifacts at the Ngoc Son Temple.
For anyone interested in learning more about Hanoi's past, these historical sites and museums are a must-visit. They offer

an extensive understanding of the city's cultural and historical legacy.

Dietary and Nutrition Guide

Hanoi's Guide to Food and Dining
Food on the Street
Vietnam's signature noodle soup, pho, is typically made with either chicken (pho ga) or beef (pho bo). Scattered across the city, including neighborhood staples like Pho Bat Dan and Pho 10.

Vietnamese baguette stuffed with an assortment of meats, veggies, and pâté is known as a banh mi. Banh Mi Pho Co. and Banh Mi 25 are two well-known locations.

Bun Cha: Noodles made from vermicelli, grilled pork, and a sweet-sour dipping sauce. Bun Cha Huong Lien is definitely a place to try.

Cha Ca (grilled fish marinated in dill and turmeric) is usually served with peanuts, fresh herbs, and rice noodles. This dish is well known from Cha Ca La Vong.

Nem Ran, or spring rolls, are vegetable, mushroom, and minced pork-filled deep-fried rolls. available in a large number of the neighborhood markets and restaurants.

Neighborhood Eateries
Quan An Ngon: Provides a delightful setting with an extensive menu of traditional Vietnamese dishes. Reputable for its fine cuisine and large menu.

Renowned for its cha ca, a speciality of Hanoi, is Cha Ca Thang Long. provides tasty food and an authentic experience.
Green Tangerine: A restaurant that serves a variety of dishes in a classy setting, fusing traditional Vietnamese food with contemporary ingredients.

Coffee shops and cafés
Egg coffee (cà phê trứng), a speciality of Hanoi made with egg yolks, sweetened condensed milk, and strong coffee, is the reason Cafe Giang is well-known.
The Hanoi Social Club is a welcoming café that serves a selection of teas, coffees, and light fare. A great place to unwind and people-watch.
Highlands Coffee: Well-known chain offering a selection of Vietnamese-style coffee drinks as well as contemporary espresso-based drinks.

Mid-Level Dining
High-quality steaks and a variety of international dishes are available at El Gaucho, an Argentine steakhouse. Recognised for its warm ambiance and first-rate service.
The Hanoi House is a modern Vietnamese eatery that specializes in using fresh ingredients and creative cooking techniques.
La Badiane: Serves French and Vietnamese food in a classy atmosphere. Well-known for its elegant meals and excellent dining experience.

exquisite dining

Home Hanoi is a great option for sophisticated fine dining in an elegant setting with an emphasis on real Vietnamese flavours. features premium ingredients on a large menu.

Owen's Steakhouse is a classy dining establishment that is well-known for its fine steaks and international cuisine.

Le Beaulieu: Situated in the luxurious Sofitel Legend Metropole Hanoi, this eatery offers fine French cuisine in an elegant atmosphere.

Food streets and markets

The lively Dong Xuan Market has a large selection of fresh produce, local snacks, and street food. A great location to try a variety of regional specialities.

Hanoi Weekend Night Market: Situated in the Old Quarter, this market offers a variety of local crafts and street food vendors. Suitable for a stroll in the evening and sampling new foods.

Ta Hien Beer Street: Known for its delicious street food and vibrant atmosphere. Perfect for savoring snacks and local beer (bia hoi) among a lively crowd.

Gourmet Dining

Northern Vietnamese cuisine is the speciality of Hanh Restaurant, which serves homestyle meals in a cozy atmosphere.

Bun Bo Nam Bo: Distinguished for its beef noodle salad prepared in the southern style, blending vivid flavors and fresh ingredients.

From sophisticated dining establishments to street food adventures, Hanoi's varied culinary scene offers something for every taste, making for a fulfilling and rich culinary experience.

Shopping and After Dark

Nightlife and Shopping in Hanoi
Buying
Old Quarter

A thriving neighbourhood well-known for its conventional stores, marketplaces, and street sellers. It is the best place to look at regional textiles, crafts, and mementos.
Highlights include the various goods available at Dong Xuan Market, the silk products on Hang Gai Street, and the distinctive handmade goods available at neighbourhood craft stores.
The Vincom Centre

This contemporary mall has a variety of local and international brands, as well as food and entertainment options.
Highlights: A variety of dining options, electronics, and upscale clothing stores.
The Plaza Trang Tien

Description: A high-end retail complex renowned for its exquisite shopping experiences and luxury brands.

Highlights include upscale clothing stores, gourmet dining options, and designer boutiques.

Hanoi's Weekend Night Market

A bustling market with a wide selection of street food, crafts, and trinkets that takes place every weekend in the Old Quarter.

Street food vendors, regional apparel, crafts, and trinkets are the highlights.

Market of Dong Xuan

The biggest market in Hanoi, renowned for its wide range of merchandise that includes apparel, accessories, and regional goods.

Highlights include reasonably priced apparel, regional snacks, and home goods.

Lotte Centre in Hanoi

A massive entertainment and retail centre featuring both domestic and foreign brands.

Highlights include a sky deck with views of the city and shopping for groceries, electronics, and clothing.

Evening Life

Beer Street in Ta Hien

Known for its bars, bia hoi (local beer), and lively atmosphere, this street is lively.

Highlights include reasonably priced beverages, street cuisine, and a lively, social atmosphere.

Hanoi Opera House

This famous site hosts a variety of cultural events, such as ballet, opera, and classical music.
Highlights: Take in a performance in a historic setting to get a taste of Hanoi's cultural scene.
Junction Bia Hoi

A well-liked spot for savouring regional beer and mingling with both residents and visitors.
Highlights: Lively crowd, fresh beer served in outdoor bars, and local snacks.
The Social Club in Hanoi

At night, this hip location features live music, while during the day it's a laid-back café.
Highlights: A wide selection of drinks and light bites, a warm atmosphere, and live performances.
Theatres and Films

Hanoi provides movie buffs and culture vultures with a wide selection of theatres and cinemas.
Highlights: The Vietnam National Drama Theatre hosts live performances, and CGV is a cinema chain that screens the newest films.
Sky Bars

Elegant bars that serve sophisticated cocktails and offer expansive city views.
Highlights: For breathtaking views and upscale cocktails, visit Top of Hanoi in the Hanoi Lotte Centre and Sky Bar at the Lotte Centre.
Venues for Live Music

Hanoi is home to an expanding live music scene that features jazz, rock, and traditional Vietnamese music performed in various venues.

Highlights: Jazz Club Hanoi for live jazz performances and Hanoi Rock City for rock music.

Hanoi provides a variety of shopping and entertainment options, catering to your interests whether they are discovering the city's cultural scene, exploring bustling markets, or enjoying a lively nightlife.

Three-and-a-half-day excursions from Hanoi

The Halong Bay

Remarkable limestone karsts and emerald waters make this UNESCO World Heritage site well-known. A well-liked spot for scenic views and boat rides.

Top attractions include swimming, kayaking, visiting fishing villages, and taking day trips to discover the bay's islands and grottoes. Along with meals, cruises frequently offer activities like hiking and cave exploration.

Travel time from Hanoi: two to three hours by bus or car.

Binh Ninh

Description: Often called "Halong Bay on land," Ninh Binh is renowned for its striking scenery, rice paddies, and historic temples.

Highlights include taking a boat ride through the Tam Coc or Trang An river systems, touring the Bich Dong Pagoda and

Phat Diem Cathedral, and travelling to the ancient capital of Hoa Lu.

Travel Time: Approximately two hours from Hanoi by bus or automobile.

Sapa

Known for its breathtaking terraced rice fields, ethnic minority villages, and milder climate, this charming town in the northern mountains is described below.

Highlights include taking in the views from Fansipan, Vietnam's highest peak, trekking through picturesque landscapes, and visiting ethnic minority villages like Cat Cat and Ta Van.

Time Spent Travelling: About 1.5 hours by train, or 5 to 6 hours by vehicle or bus.

Chua Huong Perfume Pagoda

A collection of Buddhist temples that can be reached by boat and hiking in a picturesque region with limestone hills and lush vegetation.

Highlights include taking a boat ride on the Yen River, hiking up the mountain to the main pagoda, and touring the area's temples and caves.

Travel time from Hanoi is approximately two to three hours by bus or car.

The Ceramic Village of Bat Trang

Description: A traditional village well-known for its production of pottery and ceramics. In addition to trying their hand at pottery-making, visitors can watch artisans at work.

Highlights include looking around workshops, buying handmade goods, and discovering traditional pottery methods.
Travel Time: From Hanoi, it will take you between 30 and 45 minutes by bus or vehicle.

Chau Mai
Description: Nestled between mountains, this serene valley is renowned for its scenic vistas and communities of ethnic minorities.
Highlights: Touring picturesque rice paddies, visiting traditional Thai villages, and having meals with local families in the traditional manner. It's a fantastic place to discover Vietnamese rural culture.
Trip Time: From Hanoi, it takes about three to four hours by bus or car.

Hoa Lu
Description: Offering historical sites and beautiful views, this was Vietnam's ancient capital in the tenth and eleventh centuries.
Highlights include touring the historic ruins of the former capital, taking in the views of the surrounding countryside, and visiting the legendary Dinh and Le temples.
Travel Time: Approximately two hours from Hanoi by bus or automobile.

Cu Chi Tunnels
Description: Near Ho Chi Minh City, an extensive network of subterranean tunnels used during the Vietnam War. It's noteworthy for people who might be travelling between cities even though it's not a typical day trip from Hanoi.

Highlights: Investigating the tunnels, studying the history of the war, and comprehending the Viet Cong's subterranean lifestyle.

Travel Time: From Ho Chi Minh City, two hours or so by bus or automobile.

These day trips are fantastic choices for prolonging your stay in Hanoi because they provide a variety of experiences, from historical exploration to natural beauty and cultural immersion.

Chapter 4: The Northern Highlands

The Highlands in the North
Overview
Rich in cultural legacy, ethnic diversity, and breathtaking natural scenery, Vietnam's Northern Highlands are well known. This area provides a distinctive contrast to the busy city life of Hanoi with its terraced rice fields, dramatic mountain scenery, and traditional hill tribe villages.

Principal Locations
A Sapa

This well-liked mountain town is well-known for its stunning vistas, terraced rice fields, and resident ethnic minority populations.
Walking through beautiful valleys, seeing towns like Ta Van and Cat Cat, discovering vibrant markets, and climbing Fansipan, Vietnam's highest peak, are some of the highlights.
Engaging in cultural exchanges with ethnic minorities, hiking, biking, and tasting traditional foods are some of the activities available.

Hai Giang

Winding mountain roads and deep valleys abound in this isolated province, which offers some of Vietnam's most dramatic landscapes.

Highlights: Meo Vac's traditional markets, Dong Van's Karst Plateau Geopark, and Ma Pi Leng Pass.

Activities: Hiking, taking scenic drives, discovering ethnic markets nearby, and living like a local in a village.

Hac Ha

Notable for its lively weekly market and breathtakingly beautiful surroundings in the natural world. Bac Ha provides a genuine experience because it is less visited by tourists.

Two of the city's highlights are the stunning Bac Ha Castle and the Bac Ha Market, where members of the local ethnic minority sell fresh produce and handmade goods.

Activities include checking out the local ethnic villages, going to the market, and hiking in the hills nearby.

The Mu Cang Chai

Noteworthy for its breathtakingly beautiful terraced rice fields and secluded mountainous surroundings.

Highlights: Especially beautiful during the rice-growing season are the terraced fields of La Pan Tan, Che Cu Nha, and Sam Lang.

Activities: trekking, taking pictures, and visiting traditional hill tribe villages.

Yen Bai

The province, which encompasses the picturesque Thac Ba Lake, is renowned for its traditional culture and natural beauty.

Highlights: The picturesque surroundings and boat rides available at Thac Ba Lake, as well as the surrounding rural landscapes.

Activities include going on lake boat tours, shopping in the neighborhood markets, and hiking in the hills nearby.

Experiences with Culture

Ethnic Villages: The Hmong, Dao, Tay, and Giay are among the many ethnic groups that call the Northern Highlands home. You can learn about traditional crafts and lifestyles by visiting these villages.

Local markets: Markets like Bac Ha Market are thriving hubs where people of color congregate to exchange goods, produce, and crafts, creating a lively and colorful atmosphere.

Customary Celebrations: Taking part in regional celebrations, like the Dao Festivals or the Hmong New Year, offers the chance to witness customary rituals, music, and dances.

Journey Advice

Weather: Wear layers because it can get chilly in the Northern Highlands, especially at higher elevations. September through November or March through May are the ideal times to visit.

Transport: The most common ways to get to the area are by bus or private vehicle. While other places might take longer to get to, Sapa is easily accessible from Hanoi by bus or train.

Accommodations: There are several options, from budget-friendly hostels to upscale hotels and homestays. A more immersive experience may be had by staying with local families.

The Northern Highlands are a must-visit for anyone looking for adventure and cultural immersion in Vietnam because they provide a remarkable combination of natural beauty, cultural richness, and traditional experiences.

Sapa and its Adjacent Area

Sapa and its Entire Region
summary
Nestled in Vietnam's Northern Highlands, Sapa is a charming mountain town renowned for its varied ethnic minority communities, terraced rice fields, and breathtaking scenery. Trekking, cultural exploration, and adventure are all very popular in the region surrounding Sapa because of its rich cultural experiences and beautiful natural surroundings.

Sapa
Walking and Climbing

Trekking Routes: Fansipan, Vietnam's highest peak, is a strenuous hike that begins in Sapa and ends in Cat Cat Village, Ta Van Village, and other well-known trekking destinations.
Highlights: Stunning vistas of verdant valleys, terraced rice fields, and villages home to ethnic minorities. Interactions with the Hmong, Dao, and Tay people of the area are common during trekking.

regional markets

The lively Sapa Market is where the locals sell traditional foods, textiles, and handicrafts. It's a fantastic location for local culture exploration and souvenir shopping.
Sunday markets at Bac Ha: Located a little further from Sapa, this market is well-known for its lively atmosphere and the opportunity to see a variety of ethnic groups.
Cultural Locations

Cat Cat Village is a typical Hmong village distinguished by its picturesque surroundings and age-old crafts. Tourists can take in cultural performances and learn about the customs of the area.
The Giay ethnic group's Ta Van Village is well-known for its stunning rice terraces and traditional wooden homes.
Fanshawe Mountain

Fansipan, the highest mountain in Vietnam and Southeast Asia, is referred to as "The Roof of Indochina."
Activities: The summit walk offers expansive views of the surrounding area. To reach the peak, there are two options: simpler cable car rides or strenuous multi-day treks.
the surrounding area
Chai Mu Cang

A secluded area well-known for its breathtaking terraced rice fields, especially in Sam Lang, Che Cu Nha, and La Pan Tan.
Highlights include the chance to take pictures of the terraced fields, the opportunity to visit nearby ethnic villages, and beautiful drives.
Ha Bac Ha

Recognised for its vibrant marketplace and breathtaking alpine landscape.

Highlights include the historic Bac Ha Castle with its expansive views and the Bac Ha Market, which provides an insight into local life.

Giang Ha

This province features striking scenery, such as the Ma Pi Leng Pass and the Dong Van Karst Plateau Geopark.

Highlights include scenic drives, visiting the Meo Vac and Dong Van markets, and learning about the ethnic minority cultures in the area.

Yen Bai

Reputed for its unspoiled beauty, which includes Thac Ba Lake and the surrounding rural areas.

Highlights include hiking in the surrounding hills, taking boat rides on Thac Ba Lake, and touring the local markets.

Duong Tam

A little-known region with stunning scenery and ethnic villages.

Highlights include touring ethnic villages, taking scenic drives through mountainous terrain, and discovering local marketplaces.

Journey Advice

Weather: November through March is when Sapa experiences its coolest and cloudiest days. April through October are the ideal months to go because of the clearer skies and warmer weather.

Transportation: Sapa is accessible from Hanoi by bus or train. By private vehicle or motorbike, the surrounding areas are best explored.

Accommodations: You can experience the hospitality of the area by staying in anything from luxurious hotels and homestays to affordable guesthouses.

Discovering Vietnam's highland landscapes and ethnic diversity is a compelling experience that Sapa and its environs have to offer with their diverse range of natural beauty, cultural experiences, and adventure opportunities.

Adventure and Trekking Pursuits

Paths for Trekking
Trekking in Cat Cat Village
The traditional Hmong village of Cat Cat is reached via a reasonably easy trek that passes through beautiful scenery.
Highlights: Stunning vistas of the region's terraced rice fields, traditional Hmong homes, and handcrafted goods. Opportunities to talk to Hmong people and discover more about their way of life.

Trekking Through Ta Van Village
This is a moderate trek that takes you through the terraced fields and picturesque valleys that surround Ta Van, a village belonging to the Giay ethnic group.
The traditional wooden houses, gorgeous terraced fields, and breathtaking views of the Muong Hoa Valley are the

highlights. Conversation with the Giay people and investigation of regional traditions.
Trek Fansipan Peak

The highest peak in Vietnam, Fansipan, is reached after a strenuous multi-day walk.
Trekking options range from 2 to 4 days, with varying degrees of difficulty. Highlights: Diverse flora and fauna, panoramic views from the summit, and the experience of climbing Vietnam's "Roof of Indochina."
Muong Hoa Valley Hike

This walk takes you through the Muong Hoa Valley, which is renowned for its gorgeous terraced fields and villages home to ethnic minorities.
Highlights included visits to several traditional villages, including Ta Van and Lao Chai, as well as stunning scenery and cultural insights.

Trekking the Bac Ha Market
This tour combines a walk with a visit to the Bac Ha Market, where traders from different ethnic backgrounds congregate.
Highlights include the lively market, the breathtaking mountain trails, and the opportunities to engage with the local ethnic minority.

Experiential Exercises
Climbing Up Mountains
Riding a bicycle through the untamed terrain and picturesque scenery of Sapa.

Highlights include biking through ethnic villages, terraced fields, and mountainous terrain. Routes range from easy to challenging, making them suitable for a variety of skill levels.
Climbing rocks

Rock climbing opportunities can be found in the nearby limestone karst formations for those with an adventurous spirit.
Highlights: Options for beginning and experienced climbers alike on climbing routes set within naturally occurring rock formations.
caving in

Discovering the "Dark Cave" and "Silver Waterfall," two caves in the Sapa region.
Highlights include discovering subterranean formations, exploring secret caverns, and taking in the distinctive geological features of the area.
The Zip Line

A thrilling zip-lining adventure that offers sweeping views of the surroundings.
Highlights: Seeing Sapa's breathtaking natural beauty from above while soaring over picturesque valleys and terraced fields.
Experiences with Hostels

Immersion in the way of life of ethnic minority villages through lodging with local families.
Highlights: Learning about regional customs, taking part in customary activities, and savoring home-cooked meals.

Watercraft Adventures

Visiting picturesque lakes and rivers in the area, like Thac Ba Lake or the rivers surrounding Ha Giang.
Highlights: Taking boat rides on calm waters, seeing floating villages, and taking in the area's natural splendor.
Tips for Traveling with Adventure Activities
Weather: April through October offer clearer and warmer weather, making them the ideal months for trekking and other outdoor activities.
Bring the right equipment for your trek, such as waterproof hiking boots, windbreakers, and layers of warm clothing for higher altitudes.
Guides: For trekking and other adventure activities, it is advised to hire a local guide in order to ensure your safety and improve your experience.
Health and Safety: As you hike to higher altitudes, make sure you're physically fit for the activity, drink plenty of water, and be mindful of the possibility of altitude sickness.
For both novices and experienced adventurers, Sapa and the surrounding area provide a wide variety of trekking and adventure activities. It's a top choice for outdoor exploration and immersive experiences because of the breathtaking landscapes and diverse cultural offerings.

Perspectives on Culture: Ethnic Minorities

Ethnic Minorities in the Northern Highlands: Cultural Perspectives

A diverse range of ethnic minority groups, each with unique cultures, customs, and ways of life, can be found living in Vietnam's Northern Highlands. Gaining an understanding of these groups will enhance your cultural experience and provide you with important context for exploring the area.

Mmong

The Hmong people are a well-known ethnic group in the area, distinguished by their colorful attire, elaborate needlework, and customary agricultural methods.

The Hmong people follow animism and hold distinctive spiritual beliefs. Traditional music, dance, and customs are showcased during celebrations such as the Hmong New Year.

Customs: Hmong ladies are well-known for their intricate, hand-stitched attire. The Hmong people typically reside in close-knit, multigenerational families and build their traditional homes out of bamboo and wood.

Dao (Yao)

Characteristics: The Dao people are distinguished by their ornate silver jewelry and characteristic red headdresses. Primarily residing in the highlands, they are renowned for their customs and use of herbal medicine.

Culture: Buddhism and animism are practiced by the Dao. They perform traditional dances, ceremonies, and rituals to commemorate holidays like the Lunar New Year.

Traditions: Dao women dress in ornate silver jewelry and intricately embroidered garments. Dao houses built in the traditional style frequently have thatched roofs and wooden beams.

Hey,

The Tay people, who make up the second largest ethnic group in Vietnam, are mainly found in the country's northern mountainous areas. Their traditional craftsmanship and agriculture are well-known attributes.

Culture: The Tay combine Buddhism with animism. They enjoy traditional music and dancing during festivals like the "Pong Then" festival.

Customs: The Tay community resides in stilted homes made of bamboo and wood. They are adept at crafting baskets and weaving, and their clothes frequently have elaborate patterns.

Gaiay

Located in and around the Sapa region, the Giay are a smaller ethnic group. They are renowned for leading tranquil lives and using conventional agricultural methods.

Culture: The Giay combine their worship of ancestors with animism. They emphasise agriculture and communal life in their festivals and rituals.

Traditions: Giay clothing is brightly embroidered and typically simpler than that of other groups. Usually, bamboo and wood are used to build their homes.

Muong-

Located in the northern and central regions, the Muong people are closely related to the Kinh (Vietnamese) majority. Their distinctive cultural customs and agricultural prowess are well recognised.

Culture: The Muong believe in ancestor worship and animism, and they frequently incorporate traditional music and dance into their celebrations.

Customs: Muong homes are usually constructed of wood and bamboo and are raised on stilts. They are proficient in crafts and traditional weaving.

Viral Dao

Description: Wearing elaborate silver jewelry and bright red clothing, the Red Dao are a subgroup of the Dao people.

Their culture involves the practice of animism and a strong herbal medicine tradition. They honor local spirits and ancestors with traditional dances and ceremonies during their festivals.

Customs: Red Dao ladies are renowned for their intricately stitched red headscarves. With an emphasis on communal living, their homes are frequently elevated on stilts.

Hai

The Hani people belong to an ethnic minority that is located in the northwest's highlands. Their rich cultural heritage and agricultural prowess are well known.

Culture: The Hani observe several agricultural festivals and practice animism. Folklore and oral history are deeply ingrained in their culture.

Customs: Hani garments have distinctive prints and patterns. They reside in traditional homes constructed of wood and bamboo, frequently found in picturesque terraced settings.

Conversations and Honour

Visits: Approach villages inhabited by ethnic minorities with consideration and curiosity. Prior to taking any pictures, get permission, and observe any regional traditions and customs.

Markets: You can see traditional crafts and engage with local communities at ethnic markets like Bac Ha Market. Participating in market activities can offer perceptions into everyday existence and cultural customs.

Homestays: Spending time with local families can provide an immersive cultural experience and a deeper comprehension of various ethnic customs and ways of life.

With their varied customs, colorful festivals, and distinctive ways of life, the ethnic minorities of the Northern Highlands contribute to Vietnam's rich cultural landscape. Interacting with these communities offers a purposeful means of learning about the history of the area and supporting its preservation.

Places to Stay and Eat

Accommodation and Dining Choices in the Northern Highlands and Sapa
Make accommodations
Sapa

Exquisite Hotels
Offering luxurious amenities, breathtaking views of the mountains, and a full-service spa, is Sapa Jade Hill Resort & Spa.

Near Sapa's downtown, the Victoria Sapa Resort & Spa offers tasteful accommodations, a spa, and a restaurant with panoramic views.
Mid-Scale Accommodations

Easy access to Sapa's attractions and cosy rooms with contemporary amenities can be found at the Sapa Elegance Hotel.
With views of terraced fields, Eco Palms House offers a comfortable yet traditional decor.

Cheap Accommodations
The Little Sapa Hotel is an inexpensive choice with spotless accommodations and welcoming **staff**.
Hmong Sapa Hotel: Budget-friendly lodging with an emphasis on regional experiences.
House Parties

Ethnic Village Homestays: Spend time in the community by lodging with local families in villages such as Ta Van or Cat Cat. Typical fare and narrated village tours are frequently among them.

Chai Mu Cang

Houses for guests

Located in the town center, the Mu Cang Chai Hotel offers straightforward, spotless rooms with standard amenities.

Homestay Options: A more comprehensive look into traditional rural life can be had by staying with one of the many host families in the area.

Greenhouses
With views of the well-known terraced rice fields and chances to participate in local farming activities, Rice Terrace Lodge offers cozy lodging.
Giang Ha

Hotels
Ha Giang Riverside Lodge: Features traditional décor and cozy rooms overlooking the river.
The Long Hotel: A midrange choice with contemporary conveniences and convenient access to neighborhood sights.

House Parties
Ethnic Minority Homestays: For a genuine experience and a taste of the local cuisine, stay with local families in Meo Vac or Dong Van.

Yen Bai

Hotels

The mid-range Yen Bai Hotel is conveniently located and provides basic amenities.
Near the lake, the Thac Ba Lake Hotel offers cozy lodging and beautiful views.
House Parties

Local Village Homestays: Spend time in rural areas with local families to get a taste of traditional Yen Bai culture.
Menu Selections

Sapa

Regional Food

Renowned for combining contemporary presentation with traditional Vietnamese cuisine is Cha Pa Restaurant.
Offering a range of regional and international cuisine in a welcoming atmosphere is The Hill Station Signature Restaurant.
Food on the Street

Taste local specialties like "grilled pork skewers" and "thang co," a traditional Hmong dish, from street vendors in Sapa.
Cultural Cuisine

Sample traditional cuisine from the Hmong, Dao, and Tay communities at local ethnic restaurants. Specialities include "pho" and "banh cuon."

Chai Mu Cang

Local Cuisine
Local Restaurants: Savor regional specialities at tiny, family-run eateries, such as "thit luoc" (boiled meat) and rice dishes.
Ethnic Village Meals: During homestays, savor traditional meals prepared by neighborhood families.

Giang Ha

Regional Food

Quyet Restaurant: Serves grilled specialities and "thang co," among other regional cuisines.
Restaurant Ha Giang: renowned for its regional flavors and traditional fare.
Food on the Street

Local Stalls: Taste locally produced snacks and street cuisine, such as a variety of rice and meat dishes.

Yen Bai

Local Cuisine

Offering a variety of Vietnamese and regional cuisine, Lakeview Restaurant is situated overlooking Thac Ba Lake.
Local Family-Run Restaurants: Intimate, small-scale restaurants serving straightforward, home-cooked meals.
Food on the Street

Market Stalls: Sample delicacies and specialities from regional suppliers at nearby markets.
The Northern Highlands have a variety of lodging options to suit every type of traveler, including luxurious hotels, affordable options, and homestays that provide an immersive cultural experience. Savoring the distinctive flavors of the area is made possible by the diverse selection of local and

traditional dishes available for dining, ranging from street food to more formal dining establishments.

Tips for Highland Travel

Tips for Traveling to Vietnam's Northern Highlands
Climate and Stowing
The weather in the Northern Highlands is subject to sudden changes. Because the temperature can change significantly from day to night, wear layers. Pack rain gear for sudden downpours, cozy hiking boots, and warm clothes for higher altitudes.
Altitude: In places like Sapa and Fansipan, higher elevations are often associated with colder temperatures. Even during the day, be ready for cold weather.

Security and Health
Altitude Sickness: To prevent altitude sickness, allow sufficient time for acclimatization when trekking to higher altitudes. If you are prone to altitude sickness, stay hydrated and think about taking medication.
Food and Water: To prevent contracting foodborne illnesses, drink bottled or boiling water and use caution when consuming street cuisine. Select restaurants with a high turnover rate to guarantee freshness.
Health Insurance: Make sure you have medical emergency coverage for your trip, including evacuation if necessary.

Adventure Sports and Trekking
Trekking and other adventure activities may benefit from the hiring of a local guide. Your experience can be improved by a guide because they are knowledgeable about the area, the weather, and customs.
Trail Conditions: Some trekking routes can be difficult or steep. Select the routes that best suit your level of fitness, then outfit yourself accordingly.
Permits: Find out if any unique permits are needed in order to walk in specific locations, like Fansipan or protected areas.

Cultural Awareness
Respect Local Customs: When visiting ethnic minority villages, dress modestly and get people's permission before taking pictures of them. To establish rapport and demonstrate respect, pick up a few simple phrases in Vietnamese or the local dialect.
Take Part in Local Customs: Immersion in local customs, festivals, and ceremonies can enhance your trip. Show consideration for others and abide by regional traditions.

Transport
Travel Time: Give yourself extra time to get between destinations because the roads in the Highlands can be narrow and slow. When traveling from Hanoi to Sapa or other far-off places, take into account overnight buses or trains.
Local Transport: In the Highlands, motorbikes and scooters are quite popular. They offer flexibility if riding is something you feel comfortable doing, but make sure you have the right license and safety gear.

Exchange of Information
Internet and Connectivity: Although larger towns with strong connectivity, like Sapa, may have limited or no internet access, more rural areas may not have this luxury. Carry offline guides or maps in case you experience occasional disconnection.
Language: It's possible that fewer people in rural areas speak English. It can be useful to use translation apps or pick up a few simple Vietnamese phrases.

Environmental Accountability
It is recommended to adhere to the principles of "Leave No Trace" in order to reduce your environmental impact. Be mindful of the environment, dispose of waste responsibly, and don't disturb wildlife.
Help Local Economy: To help the local economy, purchase handcrafted goods and locally produced goods. Think about using sustainable tourism techniques and booking eco-friendly lodging.

Funds and Expenses
Currency: The local unit of currency is the Vietnamese Dong (VND). Major towns such as Sapa have ATMs, but in more remote areas where banking facilities may be scarce, carry cash.
Planning your budget: Take into account the price of lodging, meals, transportation, and guides. You should plan for higher prices in tourist areas.
You can make sure that your trip to Vietnam's Northern Highlands, with its breathtaking scenery and lively cultures, is

safe, pleasurable, and respectful by adhering to these travel tips.

Chapter 5: Ha Long Bay and Cat Ba Island

The Bay of HaLong and Cat Ba Island
Ha Long Bay
summary
Renowned for its stunning limestone karst seascape and emerald waters, Ha Long Bay is a UNESCO World Heritage Site. The bay, which is in northern Vietnam, is home to more than 1,600 islands and islets that together form a striking and gorgeous scenery.

Important Features

Vacations

An essential activity to fully appreciate the splendor of Ha Long Bay. Cruises can be one-day excursions or multi-day excursions.
Highlights include swimming and kayaking opportunities, as well as breathtaking views of limestone islands and floating fishing villages.
Cave of Sung Sot

One of HaLong Bay's biggest and most spectacular caves, distinguished by its expansive chambers and distinctive rock formations.
Highlights: An exquisite two-chamber cave with intricate stalagmites and stalactites that offers breathtaking views below ground.
Island Ti Top

Known for its sandy beach and sweeping views of Ha Long Bay from its viewpoint, this island is quite popular.
Highlights include lounging on the sand, swimming in the crystal-clear waves, and hiking to the viewpoint for breathtaking views of the bay.
Island Cat Ba

The biggest island in Ha Long Bay, renowned for its varied topography that includes mountains, beaches, and forests.
The sandy beaches, lively local markets, and Cat Ba National Park are the highlights.
Operations

Swimming and Kayaking: Take a kayak tour of undiscovered beaches and lagoons, or just relax in the crystal-clear waters of the bay.
Fishing Villages: To experience local culture and traditional fishing techniques, visit floating fishing villages like Vung Vieng or Cua Van.
Journey Advice

Securing Your Dream Itinerary and Boat Type: Reserve your cruise well in advance, especially during the busiest times of the year.

Weather: October through April are the ideal months to visit HaLong Bay because of the cooler, less humid weather.

Island Cat Ba

summary

The Cat Ba Archipelago includes Cat Ba Island, which offers a combination of adventurous activities and scenic natural beauty. It is less crowded than Ha Long Bay and serves as a gateway to the Cat Ba National Park.

Important Features

Cat Ba National Park

Description: A protected area featuring unique wildlife, limestone mountains, and a variety of ecosystems.

Hiking trails, such as the one leading to the Ngu Lam Peak for sweeping views, and seeing wildlife, such as the critically endangered Cat Ba langur, are the highlights.

Shorelines

Description: There are numerous stunning beaches on Cat Ba Island.

Highlights: You can sunbathe, swim and unwind at beaches like Cat Co 1, Cat Co 2, and Cat Co 3.

Lan Ha Bay

Relative to HaLong Bay, this calmer and less frequented bay is renowned for its picturesque scenery and tranquil waters.

Highlights: Sail around small islands and beaches, take boat tours, and go kayaking.
Investigation of Caves

Cat Ba Island has a number of caves that are well worth a visit.
Highlights: Take a tour of caves like Trung Trang Cave, which is renowned for its magnificent stalagmites and stalactites.
Operations

Hiking: Discover Cat Ba National Park's trails, which offer a range of difficulty levels and picturesque vistas.
Cycling: Take a bicycle rental and tour the island's rural and coastal areas.
Local Markets: Visit the Cat Ba Town markets to learn about the customs and cuisine of the area.
Journey Advice

Transportation: Cat Ba Island is connected to the mainland by speedboats and ferries. During peak hours, schedule your transportation in advance.
Lodging: There are mid-range hotels and inexpensive guesthouses to choose from. Plan ahead for your lodging, particularly during the busiest travel seasons.
Ha Long Bay and Cat Ba Island provide a range of experiences, from leisure and cultural exchange to breathtaking scenery and outdoor activities. These locations offer travelers unforgettable experiences, whether they are sailing around the bay or discovering the island's untamed landscape.

A Visit to HaLong Bay: Boats and Tours

Cruises and Tours for Discovering Ha Long Bay
Types of Cruises
Day Boats

Description: Perfect for people with a tight schedule, these short trips usually last between four and six hours.
The bay's scenic views, trips to well-known locations like Sung Sot Cave and Ti Top Island, and optional activities like kayaking are the highlights.
Ideal For: Individuals seeking a concise synopsis of Ha Long Bay or those with limited time.

Cruises for Overnights
Cruises that provide passengers the opportunity to spend one or more nights on the boat, enabling a more immersive experience.
Highlights include the bay's extended exploration, nighttime boat activities, and the sunrise views. Swimming, kayaking, and touring floating villages are common recreational pursuits.
Ideal For: Those seeking a chance to explore the bay's less-traveled areas and a more relaxed experience.
opulent cruises

Premium cruises with roomy cabins, individualized services, and top-notch amenities.

Highlights include gourmet food, spa services, and expertly led tours. Modern designs are common in luxury boats, which offer an improved Ha Long Bay experience.

Ideal For: Those looking for a luxurious vacation with first-rate comfort and service.

Individual Cruises

Customized sailing vacations with flexible schedules and activities for families or small parties.

Highlights include exclusive boat use, individualized services, and customisable routes. Perfect for personal parties or special occasions.

Ideal For: Families or groups desiring privacy and a personalized experience.

Important Trips and Events
Island Venturing
Discover the different islands in HaLong Bay, like Cat Ba Island and the less-traveled islets.

Highlights: Stunning scenery, unusual rock formations, and beach activities available. For more seclusion and exploration, some tours make stops at isolated islands.

Cave Explorations

Description: Guided tours of the main caverns, like Heavenly Palace Cave (Thien Cung Cave) and Surprise Cave (Sung Sot Cave).

Highlights include spacious chambers, exquisite rock formations, and impressive stalactites and stalagmites. Many larger tours that include nearby islands include a stop at a cave.

Swimming & Kayaking
Activities that take place on the water to discover beaches and hidden lagoons.
Highlights: Swimming in crystal-clear bays, finding quiet spots, and canoeing through tranquil waters. frequently included in cruises lasting one or more days.
Towns That Float

Experience the local way of life by visiting floating fishing villages.
Highlights: Seeing traditional fishing techniques, interacting with local fishermen, and learning about the way of life of those who live by the water.
Views of the Sunset and Dawn

Taking in breathtaking views of the bay as the sun sets and the day breaks.
Highlights include serene mornings and evenings, picturesque landscapes, and a calm atmosphere. These experiences are often scheduled into the itinerary of cruises.

Organizing a Cruise
Arrangements
Advice: To ensure your chosen cruise and cabin type, make reservations well in advance, particularly during the busiest

travel seasons. Prior to booking, read reviews and compare itineraries.
Consolidating

Bring swimwear, sunscreen, a hat, comfortable shoes, light clothing, and sunscreen. On chilly evenings, a lightweight jacket might be necessary. Remember to bring along any personal medications and your camera.
What to anticipate

Facilities: Meals, escorted activities, and standard amenities are provided on most cruises. Gourmet dining and spa services are among the extra amenities offered by luxury cruises.
Safety: Pay attention to all the crew's safety instructions. Make sure your insurance covers activities related to the sea.
Regional Advice

Respect the environment by not littering and by keeping an eye out for the local wildlife and natural areas.
Cultural Sensitivity: Approach people you meet or see in floating villages with respect and curiosity.
Cruises and tours provide a special way to discover HaLong Bay's scenic beauty, rich cultural legacy, and tranquil surroundings. You can enjoy one of Vietnam's most famous locations in a variety of ways, whether you decide on a quick day trip or a lengthy luxury cruise.

Things to Do on Cat Ba Island

Activities on the Island of Cat Ba
HaLong Bay's Cat Ba Island is renowned for its varied scenery and outdoor pursuits. Top things to do on the island include the following:

Examine Cat Ba National Park.
Rich biodiversity, limestone mountains, and rainforests are just a few of the diverse ecosystems found in this protected area.
Tasks:
Trekking: Paths such as the one that ascends Ngu Lam Peak provide expansive vistas of the island and its environs.
Looking for rare species? Look for a variety of bird species and the critically endangered Cat Ba langur.
Venture into caverns such as Trung Trang Cave, renowned for its remarkable stalactites and stalagmites.
Appreciate the Beaches
Cat Ba Island has a number of stunning beaches that are perfect for leisurely strolls and water sports.
Seashores:
Sand beaches at Cat Co 1, 2, and 3 are ideal for swimming, tanning, and taking in the crystal-clear waters.
Bai Tu Long Beach: A more isolated location with peace and beautiful scenery.
See Lan Ha Bay
Description: Lan Ha Bay is a more tranquil and peaceful place to be, right next to Ha Long Bay.

Tasks:

Boat Tours: Take in the gorgeous islands and tranquil waters of the bay. Visits to tiny islands and floating fishing villages are frequently included in tours.

Kayaking: Discover secluded coves and beaches as you paddle through serene lagoons.

Learn About Local Markets

Description: Local markets in Cat Ba Town offer a taste of the cuisine and culture of the island.

Tasks:

Shopping: Look for fresh produce, souvenirs, and handcrafted items made in the area.

Taste-testing of Local Cuisine: Savour delicacies like seafood dishes and traditional Vietnamese snacks.

Ride a bicycle.

Hire a bike to tour the picturesque roads along the coast and across the countryside of Cat Ba Island.

Routes: Ride a bicycle through rural areas, stop at nearby villages, and take in the natural splendor of the island.

Climbing rocks

Cat Ba Island provides opportunities for rock climbing, particularly near the island's limestone cliffs and in areas like Viet Hai Village.

Activities: Climbing adventures fit for a range of abilities are available; some routes have amazing views.

Take a look at Viet Hai Village.

A historic village situated in the centre of Cat Ba National Park.

Tasks:

Discover the village, talk to the people there, and discover their customs regarding farming.

Walks along the countryside: Take leisurely strolls through the village and surrounding areas.

Fishing from a boat

Join local fishermen on a boat to learn about traditional fishing techniques.

Activities: Take part in fishing excursions and discover the methods the bay's native fishermen employ.

Unwind and visit the spa

On Cat Ba Island, a number of hotels and resorts provide spa services and relaxation options.

Activities: Take pleasure in wellness services, massages, and rest in a peaceful environment.

10. Investigate Historical Sites

Discover more about the island's past by visiting historical and cultural sites.

Sites: Take a look at locations like the Cannon Fort, which provides historical context and expansive views of Cat Ba Town and its surroundings.

For those who enjoy the great outdoors, culture, or just relaxing, Cat Ba Island has a variety of activities to choose from. Everyone can enjoy activities such as hiking in the national park, relaxing on the beaches, and exploring the local markets.

The Greatest Caves and Beaches

The Greatest Caves and Beaches on Cat Ba Island
Best Shorelines
Beach Cat Co 1.

This beach is well-known for its fine sand and clear water and is close to Cat Ba Town.
Highlights: Excellent for swimming and tanning, with gentle waves. It is conveniently located near the town and offers amenities like cafes and restrooms.
Beach Cat Co 2

Located next to Cat Co 1, Cat Co 2 is a little more peaceful and less crowded.
Highlights: A great place to unwind and take in the gorgeous surroundings. compared to Cat Co 1, provides a calmer atmosphere.
Beach Cat Co. 3

Cat Co 3 is the smallest of the three main beaches in Cat Ba Town and is renowned for its peaceful environment.
Highlights: This is a fantastic location for people looking for a quieter beach experience. It offers breathtaking views and is only a short stroll from Cat Co 2.
Bai Tu Extended Beach

Bai Tu Long Beach is more remote and less crowded than other beaches on the island. It's situated on the southeast coast.
Highlights: A serene setting, a gorgeous stretch of sand, and clear waters. Ideal for people wishing to avoid the throng.
The Beach at Tung Thu

Known for its clean sand and calm waters, this beach is quieter and more to the north of Cat Ba Town.

Standouts: Great for lounging and swimming away from the busier beaches. provides a calmer, more local experience.

Greatest Caves

Cavern of Trung Trang

Trung Trang Cave is one of the biggest and most spectacular caves on the island, and it's situated right in the middle of Cat Ba National Park.

Highlights: Boasts spacious chambers with eye-catching stalagmites and stalactites. Reachable after a brief stroll from the entrance, offering a fantastic chance to investigate subterranean formations.

Cave Dau Be

Description: Part of the Day Be Archipelago, Dau Be Cave is located in the southwest of Ha Long Bay, close to Cat Ba Island.

Highlights: Distinguished by its distinctive rock formations and stunning surroundings. frequently seen while on boat tours of HaLong Bay.

Hospital Cavern

A former military installation that is now a cave is situated close to Cat Ba Town. During the Vietnam War, it served as a covert medical facility.

Highlights: With several chambers and tunnels to explore, it offers both natural beauty and historical significance.

Heavenly Palace Cave, also known as Thien Cung Cave

Description: Known for its striking formations, this place is accessible from Cat Ba Island even though it is officially located in Ha Long Bay.
Highlights: Exhibits grand chambers with breathtaking stalagmites and stalactites, along with an intriguing past.
Bat Cave (Hang Doi)

Nestled in a secluded section of Cat Ba National Park, Bat Cave is renowned for its distinctive geological features and abundant bat population.
Highlights: Provides a more daring cave exploration experience and chances to observe bats in their natural environment.
There are numerous stunning beaches and fascinating caverns to explore on Cat Ba Island. The island offers activities for all kinds of visitors, whether their goals are to unwind on quiet sandy beaches or explore intriguing underground landscapes.

Eco-Friendly Vacation Advice

Tips for Eco-Friendly Travel to HaLong Bay and Cat Ba Island
Select Eco-Friendly Lodgings
Choose lodging establishments that put sustainability first, such as hotels and guesthouses. Seek accreditations or environmentally friendly methods like water and energy conservation, waste minimisation, and energy efficiency.

As an illustration, look for lodging options that support regional environmental initiatives, recycle, and use renewable energy sources.

Reduce Your Usage of Plastic

Description: Bring reusable things to cut down on the amount of single-use plastic you use.

Reusable water bottle, shopping bag and cutlery should be brought. Steer clear of products packaged in a lot of plastic.

Honor **natural habitats and wildlife.**

Description: Keep a safe distance from wildlife and don't interfere with their normal activities.

Advice for exploring nature: To avoid disturbing the ecosystem, do not feed animals and stay on designated trails and paths.

Encourage regional and sustainable businesses.

Select to eat at neighborhood eateries, purchase goods made by regional artists, and lend support to companies that use sustainable business methods.

Advice: Seek out restaurants with eco-friendly policies and locally sourced ingredients.

Cut Down on Water and Energy Use

Description: Reduce the amount of water and energy you use by practicing resource conservation.

Reuse towels and linens throughout your stay, cut short your showers, and turn off the lights and air conditioning when not in use are some tips.

Take the bus or an environmentally friendly vehicle.

Instead of taking a cab or a motorcycle, choose electric scooters, bicycles or public transportation.

Advice: Select environmentally friendly modes of transportation to lessen your carbon footprint while touring the island or bay.

Engage in or Lead Clean-Up Operations

To help keep natural areas clean, get involved in neighborhood projects or plan your own cleanup events.

Advice: Pack a trash bag for walks or beach outings, and dispose of waste correctly. Take part in coordinated trail or beach clean-ups.

8. Consider Cultural Sensitivities

To encourage positive interactions and the preservation of local customs and traditions, kindly observe them.

Advice to Consider: Research local traditions prior to your trip, get consent before snapping pictures, and dress respectfully when visiting historical locations.

Select Eco-Friendly Tours and Activities

Choose tour companies and events that prioritize sustainability of the environment and culture.

Advice: Choose eco-friendly tours that promote responsible wildlife observation and reduce their negative effects on the environment.

Inform Both Yourself and Others

Discover the issues surrounding the local environment, culture, and sustainability and educate others on these topics.

Advice: Educate yourself on the cultural and ecological significance of the locations you visit, and persuade other tourists to travel sustainably.

You can contribute to the preservation of Cat Ba Island and Ha Long Bay's natural beauty and cultural legacy by using these eco-friendly travel tips, guaranteeing that these locations will continue to be vibrant and accessible for upcoming generations.

Lodging and Eating

Lodging and Dining on the Island of Cat Ba
Accommodation Selections
High-end lodgings and resorts

Resort & Spa on Cat Ba Island

Description: A resort on the beach with a spa, several dining options, and opulent rooms that offer breathtaking views of the ocean.
Highlights include outdoor pools, private beach access, and top-notch service.
Monkey Island Resort

Bungalows with direct beach access are available at this environmentally friendly resort on a private island.
Highlights: Numerous water sports, a secluded location, and rustic charm.
Mid-Scale Accommodations

The Paradise Hotel Cat Ba

Comfortable rooms and easy access to nearby attractions characterize this contemporary hotel in Cat Ba Town.
Highlights: Close to beaches, in-house restaurant, and rooftop terrace.

Hotel Sea Pearl

This well-placed hotel has views of the bay, a rooftop pool, and roomy accommodations.
The staff is friendly, the location is central, and the value for the money is good.
Low-cost Accommodations

The Bungalow Hostel Le Pont

Budget-friendly hostel offering options for dorms and private bungalows.
Highlights include the lovely views, friendly atmosphere, and reasonable prices.
Cat Ba Central Hostel

Offering private rooms and dorm beds, this option is well-liked by travelers on a budget.
The hotel's prime location, spotless amenities, and vibrant common space are its highlights.
Menu Selections
Neighborhood Eateries

The restaurant Quang Anh

The restaurant specializes in seafood and serves traditional Vietnamese dishes and fresh catches.
Highlights: A large menu, welcoming staff, and a genuine local dining experience.
Green Mango

Versatile Vietnamese and international cuisine is served at this highly regarded restaurant.
Highlights: Vegetarian options, a varied menu, and an elegant atmosphere.
Dining By the Beach

Cannon Fort Restaurant & Café

This restaurant, which is close to Cannon Fort, boasts expansive views and a laid-back vibe.
Highlights: A combination of Vietnamese and Western dishes, casual dining, and fantastic sunset views.
The Oasis Pub

This beachside eatery and pub is well-known for its varied menu and relaxed atmosphere.
Highlights: Suitable for sunset cocktails, live music, and a fusion of international and local cuisine.
Markets and Street Food

The Cat Ba Night Market

A thriving marketplace providing a range of regional street cuisine, fresh seafood, and mementos.
Highlights: Indulge in classic fare like banh mi, pho, and a variety of seafood dishes.
Regional Food Carts

These stand-alone restaurants provide a quick and real taste of Vietnamese food and are dispersed throughout Cat Ba Town.

Highlights: Excellent value, tasty, and a wonderful way to sample regional cuisine.

Gourmet Dining

Delicious Dining Establishment

Offering a variety of Vietnamese and Western dishes, this place is well-liked by both locals and visitors.

Highlights: Home-cooked meals, warm service, and a cosy atmosphere.

Mona Eatery

Small, family-owned eatery renowned for its warm atmosphere and fresh seafood.

Highlights: Reasonably priced, freshly prepared food, and personalized service.

Some Advice for Eating on Cat Ba Island

Experience the Local Seafood: The fresh seafood of Cat Ba Island is highly recognised. Savor delicacies such as steamed crab, seafood hotpot, and grilled squid.

Verify Hygiene Standards: To ensure proper hygiene when consuming street food, pick crowded stands that serve freshly prepared food.

Try a Variety of Menus: Although seafood is the speciality, many restaurants also serve vegetarian fare and foreign cuisine to suit a wide range of palates.

Savor the Views: A memorable meal is enhanced by the numerous eating establishments that offer picturesque views of the bay or beaches. To improve your meal, pick a restaurant with a view.

Cat Ba Island welcomes all kinds of visitors and offers a variety of lodging and dining choices, making sure that visitors may enjoy a comfortable and pleasurable stay while discovering this stunning region of Vietnam.

Chapter 6: Central Vietnam

Beautiful scenery, energetic cities, and a wealth of cultural legacy can all be found in Central Vietnam. Here's a summary of what to see in this fascinating region of the nation, which includes historical sites and natural wonders.

Dong Nai
The city is situated near multiple UNESCO World Heritage sites and is renowned for its modern infrastructure, sandy beaches, and other attributes.
Highlights:
My Khe Beach is a lovely, lengthy strand of white sand that's perfect for tanning and swimming.
Marble Mountains: Five limestone and marble hills featuring viewpoints, caves, and temples.
Dragon Bridge: An unusual bridge with a sculpture of a dragon that spits fire on weekends.
Hoi An
A well-preserved historic town known for its lantern-lit streets and historic architecture has been inducted as a UNESCO World Heritage site.
Highlights:
Explore the Old Town, a maze of markets, temples, and historic buildings lining the narrow streets.

The Japanese Covered Bridge is a famous 18th-century bridge that represents Hoi An.

Tailor Shops: One of the many tailors in town can create custom clothing for you.

Culinary Delights: Sample regional cuisine at tradi-tional eateries and from street vendors, such as Cao Lau and Banh Mi.

Hae

Description: Famous for its historical landmarks and royal legacy, Hue was once the imperial capital of Vietnam.

Highlights:

The Imperial City served as the capital of the Nguyen Dynasty. It was a walled fortress and palace complex.

With a view of the Perfume River, the famous Thien Mu Pagoda is a seven-story structure.

Royal Tombs: See the ornate tombs of the Nguyen emperors, including the Tomb of Minh Mang and the Tomb of Khai Dinh.

Ke Bang-Phong Nha National Park

Remarkable karst landscapes and vast cave systems can be found at this UNESCO World Heritage site.

Highlights:

Phong Nha Cave: Boat access is available to one of the park's most well-known caves.

Paradise Cave: An amazing cave distinguished by its remarkable stalagmites and stalactites.

Son Doong Cave is the world's largest cave and, for those who dare, offers an amazing adventure (booking required in advance).

Nhon Quy

The city by the sea is renowned for its stunning beaches and uncrowded atmosphere.

Highlights:

Beautiful scenery and crystal-clear waters can be found at Ky Co Beach.

A craggy coastal area ideal for hiking and taking in views of the sea is Eo Gio.

Thap Doi Towers: Two Cham towers that provide an insight into the area's past architectural style.

Nha Trang

Known for its vibrant atmosphere and water sports, this beach resort is well-liked by many.

Highlights:

Nha Trang Beach is a lengthy, sandy stretch of beach perfect for swimming, water sports, and tanning.

Vinpearl Land: A resort and theme park reached by cable car situated on an island.

Ancient Hindu temples with striking architecture and historical significance are the Po Nagar Cham Towers.

Advice for Traveling to Central Vietnam

The months of February through May are the ideal times to visit Central Vietnam because of the warm, dry weather during this period. Although the rainy season, which runs from September to January, can bring typhoons and heavy rains, the summer months, which run from June to August, can be hot and muggy.

Transportation: Bus, train, and air travel to Central Vietnam are all readily available. Major hub for flights to both domestic and foreign locations is Da Nang International

Airport. Major cities are connected by trains that travel the Reunification Express line.

Cultural etiquette: When visiting places of worship, dress modestly and show consideration for local traditions. When visiting pagodas and temples, take off your shoes.

Local Cuisine: Don't miss out on sampling some of the area's specialities, such as the white rose dumplings of Hoi An, the spicy beef noodle soup Bun Bo Hue, and the turmeric noodles Mi Quang.

Accommodations: Central Vietnam has a variety of lodging options, ranging from opulent resorts to hostels that are affordable. Making reservations in advance is advised, particularly during the busiest travel seasons.

From historical exploration and cultural immersion to beach relaxation and adventure, Central Vietnam has a wide range of experiences to offer. This area offers something for every kind of traveler, whether they want to hike through national parks, explore historic towns, or enjoy immaculate beaches.

Hue the Imperial City in the past

Hue's history as the Imperial City summary

The historical and cultural hub of Vietnam, Hue, was once the country's imperial capital. From 1802 until 1945, it functioned as the Nguyen Dynasty's political, cultural, and religious hub. Vietnam's Imperial City is a vast complex of palaces, temples, walls, and gates that reflects the grandeur of the country's imperial past. It is the most notable feature of the city.

The Imperial City's Main Attractions
Kinh Thanh Citadel

The Imperial City is located inside the Citadel, a sizable fortress with a broad moat and thick walls built to fend off invaders.
Highlights: The Citadel is home to a number of royal structures and gardens, as well as the Imperial City and the Forbidden Purple City.
Gate of Ngo Mon

The imposing Ngo Mon Gate, the main entrance to the Imperial City, was built specifically for the emperor's use.
The pavilion's two stories serve as highlights, and it offers a stately entrance to the imperial grounds.
Thai Hoa Palace—the "Palace of Ultimate Harmony"

This palace functioned as the royal audience chamber and ceremonial hall for significant occasions.
Highlights: The palace is well known for its elaborate carvings, ornate architecture, and exquisitely furnished throne hall.
The Purple City that is Off Limits (Tu Cam Thanh)

Description: Only those with special permission were allowed entry to the Forbidden Purple City, the emperor and his family's private residence.

Highlights: Despite extensive damage from wars, the complex's remnants still highlight its historical significance and stunning architecture.

The Palace of Eternal Longevity, or Dien Tho Residence

Description: With multiple halls, courtyards, and gardens, this area was once home to the queen mothers.

Highlights: It features lovely pavilions and tranquil gardens that provide insight into the royal women's daily lives.

The Temple Complex of To Mieu

Ancestral worship rituals were performed in this complex of temples honoring the Nguyen emperors.

Highlights: The complex contains nine dynastic urns that exhibit exquisite craftsmanship and each represent a Nguyen emperor.

Hien Lam Pavilion

Description: A three-story building that stands tall and represents the Nguyen Dynasty's unending continuation.

Highlights: The pavilion is a tribute to the era's architectural design and royal heritage.

Duyet Thi Duong Royal Theatre

Description: Featuring traditional court music and royal performances, this theater is the oldest in Vietnam.

Highlights: Traditional Vietnamese performances provide insights into the imperial court's cultural legacy for visitors to witness.

Taking a Look Around Imperial City

Walking Tours: Embarking on a guided walking tour is a highly recommended way to discover Imperial City. These tours offer background information on the complex's history as well as in-depth details on the significance of each site.

Cyclo Rides: If you want to explore the vast grounds in a different and more relaxed way, think about renting a cyclo, which is a traditional bicycle rickshaw.

Photography: The Imperial City has a lot of beautiful places to take pictures, from the imposing gates and palaces to the serene gardens and courtyards.

Cultural Events: The Imperial City offers the chance to witness traditional music and dance performances that breathe life into the Nguyen Dynasty's cultural heritage. Don't miss this chance.

Useful Data

Hours of Operation: The Imperial City is open every day from early in the morning until the late afternoon. Seasonal variations may occur in the exact timings, so check the local schedules.

Entry Fees: There is a fee to enter the Imperial City, although seniors and students frequently receive a discount. You can buy tickets online ahead of time or at the door.

Dress Code: Although there isn't a set dress code, it is polite to visit historical and cultural sites dressed modestly.

Tours with guides: To learn more about the history and architecture of the Imperial City, think about hiring a guide from the area or taking one of the scheduled tours.

Hoi An: A Charming Old Town

**Hoi An: A quaint old town
summary**
Central Vietnam's exquisitely preserved ancient town, Hoi An, is recognised as a UNESCO World Heritage site. With a blend of Vietnamese, Chinese, Japanese, and French influences, Hoi An, known for its quaint architecture, lantern-lit streets, and rich cultural legacy, gives visitors a window into the past.

**Main Attractions in the Ancient Town of Hoi An
Ancient Architectural Designs**
With well-preserved structures dating from the fifteenth to the nineteenth centuries, Hoi An's ancient town is a living museum of architecture and culture.
Highlights: French colonial buildings, Chinese assembly halls and traditional wooden houses line the winding streets.
Overpass with Japanese Cover (Chua Cau)

The Japanese community constructed this famous bridge in the 18th century to link themselves with the Chinese quarters, and it has become a symbol of Hoi An.

Highlights: This unusual roofed structure is ideal for picturesque photos because it has a small temple attached to one side.
Tan Ky's Ancient Home

One of Hoi An's oldest and best-preserved merchant homes, featuring traditional exterior and interior design.
Highlights include the combination of Chinese, Vietnamese, and Japanese architectural styles; also, there are elaborate carvings and antique furniture.
Phuc Kien's Fujian Assembly Hall

Constructed by the Chinese inhabitants of Fujian, this assembly hall is a stunning illustration of Chinese temple design.
Highlights include an ornate gate, statues of dragons, and a stunning main hall honouring the sea goddess Thien Hau.
Central Market in Hoi An

A vibrant marketplace where you can shop for fresh produce, get a taste of delicious street food, and get a sense of local life.
Highlights: A variety of food vendors, a lively atmosphere, and a wide selection of regional handicrafts and mementos.

The Lantern Festival of Hoi An
Description: Every month, during the full moon, Hoi An is transformed into a mystical wonderland by thousands of lanterns that light up the river and streets.

Highlights: Dancing performances, traditional music, and the opportunity to throw floating lanterns into the river for good fortune.

The Temple of Quan Cong

This is a temple honoring Quan Cong, a well-known Chinese general from the Three Kingdoms era.
Highlights: It's a tranquil place for introspection with elaborate decorations, colorful altars, and serene courtyards.
Firsthand Accounts of Hoi An
bespoke stores

Hoi An is well known for its custom tailoring, which provides fine bespoke apparel at affordable costs.
Highlights: Quick turnaround times for suit, dress, and traditional Vietnamese outfit fittings.

Classes in Cooking
Hands-on cooking classes taught by local chefs teach you how to prepare Vietnamese cuisine.
Highlights: Pick up fresh ingredients from neighborhood markets and cook classic meals like banh xeo, pho, and spring rolls.
The Thu Bon River Boat Rides

Description: Take a leisurely boat ride through Hoi An along the beautiful Thu Bon River.
Highlights: The breathtaking views of the surrounding islands, countryside, and historic town are particularly lovely at sunset.
Tours for Cycling

Description: Take a bike rental and tour the neighboring villages and countryside.
Highlights include riding through rice paddies, seeing traditional craft villages, and getting a taste of Vietnamese rural life.
Eating out in Hoi An

Regional Specialities
Cao Lau: a traditional Hoi An meal consisting of noodles, pork, and crisp greens, prepared using water from historic Cham wells.
White Rose Dumplings: Light and airy prawn dumplings paired with a rich and aromatic dipping sauce.
Vietnamese baguette sandwiches called banh mi are sold by street vendors and cafés and come with a variety of fillings.

Well-known Dining Establishments
Dawn Joy
This well-known eatery serves a variety of traditional Vietnamese cuisine.
Highlights include the delectable cuisine, the cooking demos, and the welcoming environment.
Club Cargo

A bakery and restaurant by the river serving a fusion of Vietnamese and Western dishes.
Highlights include delectable pastries, stunning river views, and a diverse menu.
Food on the Street

Street vendors in Hoi An sell a wide variety of foods, from savory snacks to sweet treats. The city is well-known for its street food.

Highlights: While exploring the town, sample some sweet coconut cakes, fresh spring rolls, and grilled pork skewers.

Useful Data

Ideal Time to Visit: When the weather is mild and pleasant, February through April and August through October are the ideal times to visit Hoi An.

Transportation: A lot of the attractions in Hoi An are easily accessible by foot because the town is pedestrian-friendly. Another common mode of transportation is the motorcycle and bicycle.

Fees for entry: To access some historical locations within the old town, a ticket is needed. The ticket covers admission to several attractions and contributes to the preservation of the town's history.

Beaches and Contemporary Attractions in Da Nang

summary

Known for its gorgeous beaches, cutting-edge infrastructure, and dynamic culture, Da Nang is a bustling coastal city in Central Vietnam. Da Nang itself offers a blend of modern attractions and natural beauty that makes it a must-visit place.

It is also the gateway to the imperial city of Hue and the ancient town of Hoi An.

Da Nang beaches
The Beach at My Khe
Known for its pure white sand and crystal-clear blue waters, My Khe Beach was nicknamed "China Beach" by American soldiers serving in Vietnam.
Best for swimming, tanning, and water sports like parasailing, jet skiing, and surfing.

Non-Nuoc Beach
Non Nuoc Beach is a tranquil and scenic location situated at the base of the Marble Mountains.
Highlights: Less crowded than My Khe, it provides a tranquil environment for unwinding and lovely walks along the coast.

Beach Bac My An
A lengthy beach featuring a variety of opulent resorts and beach clubs.
Highlights: With dining options and beach bars, it's ideal for those seeking a blend of luxury amenities and leisure.

Monkey Mountain, or Son Tra Peninsula
Known for its many isolated beaches, the Son Tra Peninsula provides a more untamed and unspoiled beach experience.
Best for hiking, seeing wildlife (including monkeys), and taking in expansive views of the coast are its highlights.

Da Nang's Contemporary Attractions
Dragon Overpass

This contemporary architectural wonder, shaped like a dragon, crosses the Han River.

Highlights: A popular tourist destination, the bridge breathes fire and water in a spectacular show every weekend night.

Waterfront of Han River

The lively neighborhood with parks, cafes, and restaurants is located along the Han River.

Highlights: Enjoy river cruises, go on a vibrant night market tour, or take a leisurely stroll or bike ride along the waterfront.

Ba Na Hills

The renowned Golden Bridge, verdant gardens, and French colonial architecture characterize this hill station and resort area.

Highlights: See the French Village, cross the Golden Bridge, which is supported by enormous stone hands, and ascend the longest cable car in the world.

Marble Ranges

Described as a collection of five hills made of marble and limestone that are named after the five elements.

Highlights: Explore the caverns, tunnels, and pagodas; ascend to the summit for breathtaking views of the surrounding landscape and coastline.

The Son Tra Linh Ung Temple

This pagoda, which is situated on the Son Tra Peninsula, is the home of Vietnam's tallest statue of the Goddess of Mercy.

Highlights: The 67-meter-tall statue offers visitors a tranquil atmosphere while overlooking the sea.

Asia Park (Danang Wonders of Sun World)

A theme park featuring exciting rides and a variety of cultural experiences.
Highlights: Several cultural zones representing various Asian countries, as well as The Sun Wheel, one of the tallest Ferris wheels in the world.

Da Nang's Gastronomic Treasures
restaurants serving seafood
Fresh seafood is widely available at beachside restaurants and local eateries in Da Nang, which is well-known for it.
Highlights: Steamed prawns, seafood hotpot and grilled fish are some of the dishes to try.
Regional Specialities

Mi Quang: Noodle dish with pork, prawns and fresh herbs flavored with turmeric yellow noodles.
Banh Xeo are savory pancakes from Vietnam that are stuffed with pork, prawns and bean sprouts.
Bun Cha Ca: A local favorite, this rich and flavourful soup is made with fish cake noodles.

Contemporary Cafés and Global Cuisine
The city is home to a wide variety of contemporary eateries that serve global cuisine.
Highlights: Savour gourmet coffee, inventive desserts, and a fusion of Vietnamese and Western cuisine.
Useful Data
The months of February through May are the ideal times to visit Da Nang because of the warm, dry weather during this

period. While it may get hotter, June through August are also excellent months for beach activities.

Transportation: Flights to both domestic and foreign locations are regularly scheduled from Da Nang International Airport. Bicycles, motorbikes, and taxis can all easily traverse the city.

Accommodations: There are many different types of lodging options in Da Nang, ranging from high-end resorts and hotels to more affordable hostels and guesthouses. Making reservations in advance is advised, particularly during the busiest travel seasons.

Son of Mine: Historic Ruins

Ancient Ruins: My Son
summary

A group of historic Hindu temples known as My Son can be found in Vietnam's Quang Nam Province, roughly 70 kilometers southwest of Da Nang. The Champa Kingdom, which ruled central and southern Vietnam from the fourth to the fourteenth centuries, had My Son as a religious center. My Son is now recognised as a UNESCO World Heritage site. The spiritual and architectural splendor of the Champa civilization can be fascinatingly observed in these ruins.

Historical Significance
The Champa Kingdom

With a primary focus on the Hindu deity Shiva, My Son functioned as a prominent religious location for the Champa Kingdom.
Highlights: Built over a ten-century period, the temples display the evolution of Cham art and architecture influenced by Indian Hinduism.

A UNESCO World Heritage Site
My Son's historical, cultural, and architectural significance led to its designation as a UNESCO World Heritage site in 1999.
Highlights: The location is regarded as one of Southeast Asia's premier Hindu temple complexes, on par with Angkor Wat in Cambodia and Borobudur in Indonesia.
Features of Architecture

Temple Building Complex
My Son is made up of more than 70 temples and towers, however over the ages, many of them have been damaged or destroyed by both natural and man-made forces, such as war.
Highlights: The temples are arranged in clusters, each having a central sanctuary (kalan) encircled by smaller structures and towers.

Building with Brick and Stone
The temples were built with sandstone and reddish bricks, and they have elaborate bas-reliefs and carvings that show Hindu gods, scenes from mythology, and floral designs.
Highlights: One of the sites architectural mysteries is the way that bricks are bonded together without the use of mortar.
The Temple of Bhadreshwara

One of the most important and ancient buildings, honoring Bhadreshwara, a manifestation of Shiva.
Highlights: The temple is regarded as a masterpiece of Cham architecture and has stunning carvings.

Principal Points of Interest
B, C, and D Temple Groups
At My Son, these groups are home to some of the oldest and best-preserved temples.
Highlights: The ornately decorated gateways and tower sanctuaries of Group B are especially noteworthy.

Temples of Group A
Once the most magnificent buildings at My Son, the Group A temples suffered significant damage in the Vietnam War.
Highlights: These temples' ruins still shed light on the opulence of Cham architecture despite their damage.
Group G Temples

The intricate carvings and sculptures found in these temples make them noteworthy.
Highlights: Group G's elaborate depictions of Hindu deities and motifs demonstrate the artistry and skill of Cham craftsmen.

Seeing My Son
Tours with a guide
Take a guided tour to get a deeper understanding of My Son's cultural and historical background.

Points of interest: Skilled tour guides give thorough explanations of the historical significance of each temple and the Champa civilisation.

The Ideal Time to Go
In order to escape the midday heat, it is ideal to visit My Son in the early morning or late afternoon.
Highlights: You can also enjoy a more tranquil and less congested atmosphere when you visit during these times at the ruins.
Exhibitions of Culture

Description: The location offers a rich cultural experience with regular traditional Cham music and dance performances.
Highlights: The lively cultural legacy of the Cham people is shown through these performances.

Capturing Images
With its breathtaking temple ruins set against verdant hills, My Son offers a plethora of photographic opportunities.
Highlights: Take in all of the fine details of the carvings and the tranquil beauty of the surroundings.

Useful Data
Reaching My Goal
Transportation: You can travel to My Son from Da Nang and Hoi An by car, motorcycle or tour bus that is arranged. From either city, the trip takes about one and a half hours.
Tours: A lot of travel agencies in Da Nang and Hoi An provide half-day or full-day tours to My Son, which are frequently coupled with visits to other locations nearby.

Entrance Charges
The temples and museum are accessible to those who pay the admission fee to enter the My Son site.
Highlights: A portion of the fee goes towards maintaining and preserving the historical site.
Visitor Centres

The location provides standard amenities like lavatories, a visitor center, and a small museum with artifacts and details about My Son.
Highlights: More history and context about the Champa Kingdom and its architectural accomplishments are provided by the museum.

Clothing Guidelines and Protocols
Because My Son is a site with spiritual and historical significance, please dress respectfully and modestly.
Highlights: Because the terrain can be uneven and require some climbing, wear comfortable walking shoes.

Cultural Celebrations and Occasions

Festivals and Events of Culture

summary

Vietnam boasts an extensive array of cultural festivals and events that aptly showcase its multifarious legacy and customs. These festivals provide distinctive insights into the Vietnamese way of life, ranging from traditional celebrations based on folklore to more recent events showcasing modern culture.

Principal Celebrations and Occasions
Lunar New Year, or Tet Nguyen Dan

Tet, which commemorates the lunar new year and the arrival of spring, is the most significant and extensively observed holiday in Vietnam.

Highlights: Gatherings of family, special dishes like banh chung (square sticky rice cake), and customs like exchanging "li xi" (lucky money). Vibrant flowers and lanterns adorn the streets, and a multitude of public events, such as parades and fireworks, take place.

Tet Trung Thu, or the Mid-Autumn Festival

The Mid-Autumn Festival, observed on the fifteenth day of the eighth lunar month, is a time for kids' activities and family get-togethers.

Highlights include the lion dances, lantern processions, mooncakes, and kid-performed events. Families gather to enjoy games and feasts while taking in the sight of the full moon.

Festival of Hue

Held every two years in the former imperial capital of Hue, this event honors the rich cultural legacy of the city.

Highlights include dragon boat races, royal court music, traditional music and dance performances, and exhibitions. With intricate displays and reenactments, the festival seeks to bring back the historical and cultural elements of the Nguyen Dynasty.

The Lantern Festival of Hoi An
Held in the historic town of Hoi An on the fourteenth day of each lunar month, this festival turns the town into a mystical flurry of lights.
The street lights with lanterns, the riverside lanterns, the traditional dance and music, and the regional cuisine are the highlights. It honors the town's historical beauty and is a calm and magical experience.
Le Hoi Chua Huong, the Perfume Pagoda Festival

Held from January to March at the Perfume Pagoda in Hanoi, this is one of the biggest Buddhist pilgrimages in Vietnam.
Highlights: Travelers ascend mountains, take boats along the Yen Stream, and stop at temples and pagodas to offer prayers for prosperity and good health. The trip is a picturesque and spiritual experience that draws thousands of tourists.

International Fireworks Festival in Danang
An annual event held in Da Nang that features international teams competing in a spectacular fireworks competition over the Han River.
Highlights include cultural events, musical fireworks displays, and a variety of riverbank entertainment options. A highlight of the city's cultural calendar, the event draws sizable crowds.

Day of the Vietnamese Nation
commemorates the nation's 1945 declaration of independence from French colonial rule and is observed on September 2nd. Highlights include patriotic displays across the nation, parades, and fireworks. Public celebrations are held in major cities such as Hanoi and Ho Chi Minh City, which include cultural performances, music, and dance.

The Cau Ngu Festival
Coastal communities, especially those in the central provinces, celebrate a customary fishing festival.
Highlights: Boat races, folk games, and ceremonies to honor the Whale God and pray for a successful fishing season. A strong bond between the sea and the surrounding communities is reflected in the festival.

Festival of Lim
This event honors the customary Quan Ho folk singing and is held in the province of Bac Ninh.
Highlights: A variety of traditional games and activities, as well as performances of Quan Ho singing, an intangible cultural heritage recognised by UNESCO. A lively celebration of regional music and culture, it is.

Vu Lan, or Wandering Souls Day
Description: Celebrated on the 15th day of the 7th lunar month to honor deceased ancestors, this event is also known as the Ghost Festival.
Highlights: Eating meals and giving symbolic paper objects to ancestors, going to pagodas, and carrying out ceremonies to soothe stray animals

Chapter 7: Vietnam's Hidden Gems

Vietnam's Hidden Gems
Overview
While Vietnam's popular destinations like Hanoi, Ho Chi Minh City, and Ha Long Bay draw many visitors, the country is also home to numerous hidden gems. These lesser-known spots offer unique experiences, stunning landscapes, and rich cultural insights, providing a more intimate look at Vietnam's diverse heritage.

Northern Vietnam Hidden Gems
Ban Gioc Waterfall
Description: Located on the border between Vietnam and China, Ban Gioc is one of the most beautiful waterfalls in Vietnam.
Highlights: The falls are surrounded by lush greenery and karst mountains. It's a great spot for photography and peaceful picnics.
Ba Be National Park

Description: A stunning natural reserve featuring Ba Be Lake, waterfalls, caves, and diverse wildlife.
Highlights: Explore the lake by boat, hike through the park's trails, and visit ethnic minority villages.

Mu Cang Chai

Description: Known for its picturesque terraced rice fields, Mu Cang Chai offers breathtaking landscapes and cultural experiences.
Highlights: Visit during the rice harvesting season (September to October) for stunning views, and stay in local homestays to learn about the Hmong culture.

Central Vietnam Hidden Gems
Phong Nha-Ke Bang National Park
Description: A UNESCO World Heritage site, this park is home to some of the world's largest and most spectacular caves.
Highlights: Explore the Son Doong Cave, the largest cave in the world, and visit other incredible caves like Phong Nha and Paradise Cave.

Tam Coc
Description: Often referred to as "Ha Long Bay on land," Tam Coc features limestone karst landscapes and serene waterways.
Highlights: Take a boat ride through the Ngo Dong River, visit the Bich Dong Pagoda, and cycle through the peaceful countryside.

Off-the-Beaten-Path Destinations

Off-the-Beaten-Path Destinations
Overview

Vietnam is a land of stunning landscapes and rich culture, with many destinations that remain relatively untouched by mass tourism. These off-the-beaten-path locations offer unique experiences, serene environments, and a deeper connection to local traditions and nature. Here are some of the best hidden spots to explore.

Northern Vietnam
Ha Giang
Description: Known for its rugged mountains and ethnic diversity, Ha Giang is perfect for adventurous travelers seeking stunning scenery and cultural immersion.
Highlights: Ride the Ha Giang Loop on a motorbike, visit the Dong Van Karst Plateau Geopark, and experience local life in ethnic minority villages such as the Hmong and Tay.
Cao Bang

Description: This province is home to the magnificent Ban Gioc Waterfall and a landscape dotted with karst mountains and lush valleys.
Highlights: Explore the Ban Gioc Waterfall, visit the Nguom Ngao Cave, and learn about Vietnam's history at Pac Bo Cave where Ho Chi Minh lived.

Yen Bai
Description: Famous for its terraced rice fields, particularly in Mu Cang Chai, Yen Bai offers breathtaking views and cultural experiences.
Highlights: Trek through the rice terraces, stay with local families in traditional stilt houses, and visit the Thac Ba Lake for boating and fishing.

Central Vietnam
Quang Binh
Description: Home to the Phong Nha-Ke Bang National Park, Quang Binh boasts spectacular caves and untouched nature.

Highlights: Explore the Son Doong Cave, visit Phong Nha and Paradise Caves, and enjoy the serene Chay River and Toi Cave (Dark Cave).

Binh Dinh

Description: This coastal province features beautiful beaches, historical sites, and a relaxed atmosphere away from the crowds.

Highlights: Visit Ky Co Beach, explore the ancient Champa ruins of Banh It Towers, and enjoy fresh seafood in Quy Nhon.

Kon Tum
Description: Known for its indigenous culture and beautiful landscapes, Kon Tum offers a unique experience in Vietnam's Central Highlands.

Highlights: Visit the wooden Kon Tum Cathedral, explore the traditional Rong houses of the Bahnar people, and trek through the forests of Chu Mom Ray National Park.

Southern Vietnam

An Giang
Description: Situated in the Mekong Delta, An Giang is known for its diverse cultures and picturesque landscapes.

Highlights: Visit Tra Su Cajuput Forest, explore Sam Mountain and the Ba Chua Xu Temple, and experience the floating markets of Long Xuyen.

Bac Lieu
Description: This province offers a mix of cultural heritage and natural beauty, with less tourist traffic.
Highlights: See the Bac Lieu Wind Farm, visit the historic Bac Lieu Prince's House, and explore the Xiem Can Pagoda.

Soc Trang
Description: Soc Trang is known for its rich cultural diversity, including Khmer, Chinese, and Vietnamese communities.
Highlights: Visit the colorful Chua Doi (Bat Pagoda), see the Kinh Bac Pagoda, and enjoy the lively atmosphere of the Nga Nam Floating Market.

Unique Cultural Experiences
Pu Luong Nature Reserve
Description: Located in Thanh Hoa Province, this reserve features stunning rice terraces and traditional villages.
Highlights: Trek through lush landscapes, stay in eco-lodges or homestays, and experience the culture of the Thai and Muong ethnic groups.

Mai Chau
Description: A tranquil valley surrounded by mountains, Mai Chau is known for its traditional stilt houses and vibrant culture.

Highlights: Stay with a local family in a stilt house, bike through rice paddies, and enjoy traditional Thai music and dance performances.

Practical Information
Best Time to Visit
Description: The ideal time to visit these off-the-beaten-path destinations varies by region but generally falls between November and April.
Highlights: Northern highlands are best visited in spring (March-April) or autumn (September-October), while the central and southern regions are pleasant during the dry season (November-April).

Transportation
Description: Reaching these destinations often involves a combination of flights, buses, and motorbike rentals.
Highlights: Domestic flights can take you to nearby major cities, from which you can continue by bus or motorbike to more remote areas.

Accommodation
Description: Options range from local homestays and guesthouses to eco-lodges and small hotels.
Highlights: Staying in homestays enhances the cultural experience and supports local communities. Eco-lodges offer comfortable amenities while maintaining sustainability.

Lesser-Known Cultural Experiences

Overview
Vietnam is a country rich in cultural heritage, with many lesser-known experiences that offer unique insights into its diverse traditions, arts, and lifestyles. These hidden cultural gems provide an opportunity to delve deeper into Vietnam's vibrant and varied cultural tapestry.

Northern Vietnam
Ethnic Minority Festivals in Ha Giang
Description: Ha Giang Province is home to several ethnic minority groups, each with its own distinct festivals and traditions.
Highlights: Attend the Hoang Su Phi Rice Festival, where locals celebrate the harvest with traditional dances and music, or visit during the Lunar New Year (Tet) to experience cultural performances and rituals.

Traditional Craft Villages in Hanoi
Description: Hanoi is surrounded by villages known for their traditional crafts, offering a glimpse into local artisan techniques.
Highlights: Visit Bat Trang Ceramic Village to see pottery-making demonstrations, or explore Dong Ho Village for traditional woodblock printing and folk art.

Cao Bang's Ethnic Culture

Description: Cao Bang Province features a rich mix of ethnic cultures and traditions, often overlooked by mainstream tourism.

Highlights: Experience the traditional lifestyle of the Tay and H'mong people, visit their local markets, and witness traditional weaving and embroidery techniques.

Central Vietnam
Cham Culture in My Son

Description: My Son is an ancient Cham site that offers a unique insight into the Cham civilization that once thrived in central Vietnam.

Highlights: Explore the ancient Hindu temples and towers, attend traditional Cham dance performances, and learn about the history and significance of Cham art and architecture.

Hue's Royal Cuisine

Description: Hue, the former imperial capital, is known for its distinctive royal cuisine, which remains largely undiscovered by many tourists.

Highlights: Sample traditional dishes such as Banh Khoai (Hue-style pancakes) and Bun Bo Hue (spicy beef noodle soup) at local eateries, and visit cooking classes to learn royal recipes

Local Markets and Villages in Hoi An

Description: Beyond the historic town of Hoi An, there are lesser-known markets and villages that showcase traditional crafts and lifestyles.

Highlights: Explore Thanh Ha Pottery Village to see traditional ceramics being made, and visit Tra Que Herb

Village to learn about organic farming and traditional Vietnamese herbs.

Southern Vietnam
Cao Dai Religion in Tay Ninh
Description: Tay Ninh is the center of the Cao Dai religion, a unique Vietnamese faith that blends elements from various world religions.
Highlights: Attend a Cao Dai ceremony at the Cao Dai Holy See, explore the colorful temple with its eclectic mix of architectural styles, and learn about the religion's history and beliefs.

Khmer Culture in Soc Trang
Description: Soc Trang is home to a significant Khmer community, with rich cultural traditions and unique temples.
Highlights: Visit the beautiful Khmer pagodas such as Chua Doi (Bat Pagoda), and experience traditional Khmer festivals and dances, such as the Water Festival.

Traditional Boat Life in Ben Tre
Description: Ben Tre, a province in the Mekong Delta, offers a glimpse into the traditional boat-based lifestyle of the local people.
Highlights: Take a boat ride through the Mekong Delta's canals, visit local coconut farms, and observe traditional crafts like coconut candy-making and mat weaving.

Unique Cultural Insights
Local Festivals in Con Dao Islands

Description: The Con Dao Islands are known for their peaceful atmosphere and unique local festivals.
Highlights: Attend the Con Dao Island Festival, which celebrates local culture and traditions with music, dance, and traditional ceremonies.

Tet Trung Thu (Mid-Autumn Festival) in Rural Areas

Description: The Mid-Autumn Festival, or Tet Trung Thu, is widely celebrated across Vietnam but has unique local variations in rural areas.
Highlights: Experience the festival in a rural village to see traditional lantern parades, lion dances, and mooncake-making activities.
Traditional Music and Dance in Dalat

Description: Dalat offers opportunities to experience traditional Vietnamese music and dance in a picturesque setting.
Highlights: Attend performances of traditional Vietnamese folk music and dance at local cultural centers, and explore the city's French colonial architecture and gardens.

Practical Information
Best Time to Visit
Description: Cultural festivals and local events occur throughout the year, so timing your visit can enhance your experience.
Highlights: Check local festival calendars and plan your visit around major cultural events or festivals to fully immerse yourself in Vietnamese traditions.

Local Guides and Tours

Description: Engaging with local guides or tour operators can provide deeper insights into cultural practices and ensure a more authentic experience.

Highlights: Look for tours that focus on cultural immersion, traditional crafts, and local festivals for a more enriching travel experience.

Respecting Local Traditions

Description: Understanding and respecting local customs and traditions is essential when visiting cultural sites and participating in local festivals.

Highlights: Dress modestly when visiting temples or participating in ceremonies, ask for permission before taking photos, and follow local customs and etiquette.

Unique Activities and Adventures

Overview

Vietnam's diverse landscapes and rich culture offer a wide array of unique activities and adventures that cater to thrill-seekers and culture enthusiasts alike. From exploring remote regions to engaging in traditional practices, these activities provide an authentic and exhilarating way to experience the country.

Northern Vietnam

Motorbiking the Ha Giang Loop

Description: This adventurous loop takes you through some of Vietnam's most stunning mountainous landscapes and ethnic minority villages.
Highlights: Enjoy breathtaking views of terraced rice fields, rugged mountains, and picturesque valleys. Interact with local communities and experience traditional village life.

Trekking in Sapa
Description: Sapa's terraced rice fields and ethnic minority villages offer excellent trekking opportunities.
Highlights: Trek through scenic trails, visit remote villages like Lao Chai and Ta Van, and enjoy stunning vistas of the Hoang Lien Son mountain range. Stay with local families for an immersive experience.

Caving in Phong Nha-Ke Bang National Park
Description: Home to some of the world's largest and most spectacular caves, this park is a haven for caving enthusiasts.
Highlights: Explore the Son Doong Cave, the world's largest cave, or the stunning Paradise Cave. Go on guided tours to navigate the intricate cave systems and marvel at the underground landscapes.

Central Vietnam
Exploring the Ancient Cham Ruins of My Son
Description: My Son is an ancient Hindu temple complex that offers a glimpse into the Cham civilization.
Highlights: Wander through the ruins of My Son, learn about Cham culture and history, and enjoy traditional Cham dance

performances. The site provides a unique perspective on Vietnam's ancient heritage.

Mountain Biking in Da Nang

Description: Da Nang offers a variety of trails for mountain biking enthusiasts looking for an off-road adventure.
Highlights: Ride through scenic trails in the Ba Na Hills, tackle the challenging routes of the Marble Mountains, and enjoy coastal views along the Hai Van Pass.

Hot Air Ballooning Over Hue
Description: Experience the historic city of Hue from a unique vantage point with a hot air balloon ride.
Highlights: Soar above the ancient citadel, tombs, and surrounding landscapes of Hue. Enjoy panoramic views of the Perfume River and the lush countryside.

Southern Vietnam
Kayaking in the Mekong Delta
Description: Explore the Mekong Delta's intricate waterways and lush landscapes by kayak.
Highlights: Paddle through serene canals, visit floating markets, and observe local life along the river. Experience the natural beauty and cultural richness of the delta up close.

Exploring the Cu Chi Tunnels
Description: These extensive underground tunnels offer a fascinating look at Vietnam's wartime history.
Highlights: Explore the maze of tunnels used by the Viet Cong during the Vietnam War. Learn about the strategies and

hardships of the war, and experience the historical significance of the site.

Snorkeling and Diving in Con Dao Islands

Description: The Con Dao Islands are known for their pristine marine environments and excellent snorkeling and diving opportunities.
Highlights: Discover vibrant coral reefs, swim with tropical fish, and explore the underwater ecosystems of the Con Dao Marine Park. Enjoy the tranquility of the secluded islands.
Unique Cultural Experiences

Traditional Weaving Workshops in Hoi An

Description: Hoi An is known for its traditional weaving practices, and participating in a workshop offers a hands-on cultural experience.
Highlights: Learn the art of traditional weaving from local artisans, create your own woven items, and understand the cultural significance of weaving in Vietnamese heritage.

Participating in a Vietnamese Cooking Class

Description: Vietnamese cuisine is renowned for its flavors and techniques. Joining a cooking class provides insight into traditional culinary practices.
Highlights: Visit local markets to select fresh ingredients, learn how to prepare classic dishes such as Pho and Banh Xeo, and enjoy a meal of your own creation.

Participating in a Local Festival
Description: Vietnam's numerous festivals provide a vibrant and immersive cultural experience.
Highlights: Attend festivals such as Tet Trung Thu (Mid-Autumn Festival) in rural areas, the Hoi An Lantern Festival, or the Cao Dai Holy See ceremonies in Tay Ninh. Experience traditional music, dance, and local customs.

Adventure and Nature Activities
Zip Lining in Dalat
Description: Dalat's beautiful landscapes offer thrilling zip-lining opportunities.
Highlights: Soar above the lush forests and picturesque valleys of Dalat, enjoying spectacular views and an adrenaline-pumping adventure.

Hiking to Ba Na Hills
Description: The Ba Na Hills, located near Da Nang, offer various hiking trails with breathtaking views.
Highlights: Trek through dense forests and along scenic paths, reaching the famous Golden Bridge with its giant stone hands. Explore the sprawling Ba Na Hills resort and enjoy panoramic views.
Cycling in the Mekong Delta

Description: Cycling through the Mekong Delta provides an active way to explore its scenic landscapes and vibrant local life.
Highlights: Ride through rural villages, explore lush green fields, and visit traditional markets and local homes.

Experience the daily life and natural beauty of the delta at a leisurely pace.

Practical Information
Best Time to Visit
Description: The ideal time for adventure activities depends on the region and the season.
Highlights: Generally, the dry season (November to April) is best for most outdoor activities, though certain regions may have different peak times.
Safety and Preparation

Description: Ensure safety by choosing reputable operators for adventure activities and being prepared for varying weather conditions.
Highlights: Wear appropriate gear, follow safety instructions, and check weather forecasts before engaging in outdoor adventures.
Local Guides and Tours

Description: Local guides can enhance your adventure experience with their expertise and local knowledge.
Highlights: Consider booking guided tours for activities like caving, trekking, and cultural workshops to ensure a safe and enriching experience.

Local Insights and Tips

Overview

Navigating Vietnam's diverse regions and cultures can be an enriching experience with the right local insights and tips. Understanding local customs, practical travel advice, and cultural nuances will enhance your journey and help you connect more deeply with the country.

Local Customs and Etiquette
Respect for Traditions

Description: Vietnam has a rich tapestry of traditions and customs, many of which are observed in daily life and during special occasions.
Tips: Dress modestly, especially when visiting temples and religious sites. Remove your shoes before entering homes and temples, and avoid touching people on the head, which is considered sacred.

Greetings and Communication

Description: The Vietnamese are friendly and polite, with specific customs for greetings and communication.
Tips: A handshake is common, but be gentle. Use both hands when giving or receiving something, and address people by their titles and surnames.

Dining Etiquette

Description: Meals are an important part of Vietnamese culture, with specific customs for dining.
Tips: Wait for the oldest person to start eating before you begin. Use chopsticks properly and avoid sticking them

upright in your bowl, as this resembles incense sticks used in funerals.
Practical Travel Tips

Currency and Payments
Description: Vietnam's currency is the Vietnamese Dong (VND), and cash is widely used.
Tips: Carry cash for small purchases and street food. Credit cards are accepted in larger establishments. Use ATMs or exchange services for cash, and be aware of potential transaction fees.

Transportation
Description: Vietnam offers various transportation options, from motorbikes to trains.
Tips: Use ride-hailing apps like Grab for convenient transportation in cities. For long distances, consider trains or buses. Be cautious when renting motorbikes, and always wear a helmet.

Language and Communication
Description: Vietnamese is the official language, but English is spoken in tourist areas.
Tips: Learn basic Vietnamese phrases to enhance your interactions. Carry a translation app or phrasebook to help with communication in more remote areas.

Food and Dining
Street Food
Description: Street food is a staple of Vietnamese cuisine, offering delicious and affordable options.

Tips: Choose vendors that are busy and have high turnover to ensure freshness. Try local specialties like Pho, Banh Mi, and fresh spring rolls.

Food Safety
Description: While street food is generally safe, it's important to be mindful of food hygiene.
Tips: Drink bottled or filtered water, avoid ice from street vendors, and choose cooked foods over raw items.

Dining Experience
Description: Dining in Vietnam is often a communal experience, with a variety of dishes shared among the group.
Tips: Be open to trying new dishes and flavors. Share meals family-style and enjoy the variety of flavors that Vietnamese cuisine offers.

Cultural Insights
Festivals and Events
Description: Vietnam celebrates numerous festivals throughout the year, reflecting its diverse cultural heritage.
Tips: Attend local festivals such as Tet (Lunar New Year), the Mid-Autumn Festival, or regional celebrations to experience Vietnamese culture firsthand. Check local event calendars to coincide your visit with a festival.

Shopping and Bargaining
Description: Markets and shops often involve bargaining, especially in local markets.

Tips: Don't hesitate to negotiate prices in markets. Start with a lower offer and be prepared to walk away if the price doesn't meet your budget.

Safety and Health
Description: Vietnam is generally safe for travelers, but taking precautions is important.
Tips: Use mosquito repellent to avoid insect-borne diseases. Be cautious with street food and drink bottled water. Keep your belongings secure and be aware of your surroundings, especially in crowded areas.
Local Recommendations

Hidden Gems
Description: Beyond popular tourist sites, Vietnam has many lesser-known attractions.
Tips: Explore off-the-beaten-path destinations such as the Con Dao Islands, Ba Be Lake, or rural areas in the Mekong Delta for a unique experience.

Local Guides
Description: Engaging local guides can enhance your travel experience with insider knowledge.
Tips: Hire local guides for personalized tours and insights into regional customs, history, and hidden spots.

Cultural Respect
Description: Respecting local customs and practices enhances your experience and interaction with locals.

Tips: Learn about local customs before visiting specific regions. Be courteous and considerate in your interactions with local communities.

Frequently asked questions

What time of year is ideal for travel to Vietnam?
The optimal time to visit Vietnam depends on where you are going. In general, the best seasons for weather are spring (February to April) and autumn (September to November). While central Vietnam enjoys a more consistent climate, northern Vietnam is characterized by harsh winters and scorching summers. With a rainy season spanning from May to October, southern Vietnam experiences year-round warmth.

Is a visa required for travel to Vietnam?
In most cases, a visa is required for entry into Vietnam. But for a limited time, certain nationalities are allowed entry without a visa. Verifying the necessary visa for your country of residence and length of stay is crucial. For travelers who meet the requirements, they can apply for an e-visa online or through the Vietnamese embassy or consulate.

What is the accepted form of payment in Vietnam, and where can I exchange money?
In Vietnam, the Vietnamese Dong (VND) is the currency in use. Airports, banks, and authorized exchange offices all offer currency exchange services. There are plenty of ATMs in large cities and towns where you can get cash out.

Is visiting Vietnam a safe option?

In general, traveling to Vietnam is safe. In crowded places, small-time crimes like pickpocketing can happen. It's critical to be mindful of your possessions, travel in a reliable manner, and heed any safety and health recommendations from the area. For the most recent information, review travel advisories prior to your trip.

Which tongue is used in Vietnam?
The official language is Vietnamese. In restaurants, hotels, and tourist destinations, English is widely spoken. Gaining some basic Vietnamese language skills will improve your trip, particularly in more rural regions.

What should I bring with me to Vietnam?
In response to the hot and muggy weather, bring lightweight, breathable clothing. Don't forget the bug repellent, sunscreen, and hat. Carry warmer clothing if you're visiting the north in the winter. A tiny first-aid kit, reusable water bottle, and comfy walking shoes are also advised.

How do I travel throughout Vietnam?
In Vietnam, you can travel by domestic airlines, taxis, trains, buses, motorbikes, and ride-hailing applications. In urban areas, there are bus and cyclo options for public transportation. Renting a motorbike or going on guided tours are good options for rural locations.

What are Vietnam's primary points of interest?
The imperial city of Hue, Ha Long Bay, Sapa, Hoi An Ancient Town, the Mekong Delta, and the Cu Chi Tunnels are some of

the major attractions. Every area has distinctive natural and cultural experiences to offer.

How is the cuisine in Vietnam prepared?
Response: The cuisine of Vietnam is rich and varied, offering items like spring rolls, banh mi (a sandwich), pho (noodle soup), and other rice and seafood dishes. Popular street food provides a true taste of regional flavors.

Is it necessary for me to take any health precautions before visiting Vietnam?
For advice on recommended immunisations and safety measures, speak with your healthcare provider. Hepatitis A and B, typhoid, and tetanus vaccinations are frequently administered. To prevent foodborne infections, it's also a good idea to apply insect repellent, drink bottled or boiling water, and exercise caution when eating street food.

How do I get internet access in Vietnam?
In hotels, restaurants, and public areas, internet access is commonly provided by Wi-Fi. Renting a mobile hotspot can provide dependable connectivity, or you can purchase a local SIM card for phone and data services.

What is customary and etiquette in the area that I should be aware of?
One way to show respect for local customs is to take off your shoes before entering homes or places of worship and to dress modestly when visiting temples. In your interactions, act courteous and thoughtful, and refrain from making public shows of affection.

How Can I Steer Clear of Travel Scams?
Reactions that seem too good to be true or people who are extremely friendly should be avoided. For travel and tours, use reliable service providers, and make sure you are comfortable with the costs before reserving any services. Remain aware of typical con games in the region you are visiting.

What is the custom of leaving tips in Vietnam?
In response, leaving a tip is appreciated but not required. It is customary in restaurants to leave a small amount (approximately 5–10% of the bill) or to round up the bill. A small gratuity based on the level of service rendered is also appreciated for hotel staff and tour guides.

How should I respond to an emergency?
Answer: Get in touch with your embassy or the local authorities in an emergency. Keep a copy of your most important documents on you and keep a list of emergency contacts. In case of an emergency, visit the closest hospital or clinic to get assistance.

Conclusion

Traveling through Vietnam is a truly enriching and diverse experience, combining vibrant cities, rich cultural heritage, and breathtaking natural landscapes. Every traveler can expect an unforgettable experience in Vietnam, from the vibrant streets of Hanoi to the serene waters of Ha Long Bay, and from the historic charm of Hoi An to the vibrant energy of Ho Chi Minh City.

You can make sure that your visit is both pleasurable and considerate of the environment and culture by organizing it with local customs and environmentally friendly activities in mind. Take steps to reduce your ecological footprint, support neighborhood-based projects, and embrace regional customs.

Vietnam welcomes you to discover its distinct fusion of the old and the new, whether you're exploring historical sites, indulging in mouthwatering cuisine, or finding hidden gems. Your trip through Vietnam will not only be a memorable experience for you, but it will also benefit this stunning nation if you plan ahead and travel with awareness.

Enjoy your trip through Vietnam and be careful of the roads!

Printed in Great Britain
by Amazon